How to Read the Apocalypse

Jean-Pierre Prévost

# How to Read the Apocalypse

CROSSROAD · NEW YORK

1993
The Crossroad Publishing Company
370 Lexington Avenue, New York, N.Y. 10017

Translated by John Bowden and Margaret Lydamore from the French
*Pour Lire L'Apocalypse*
published 1991 by Novalis and Les Editions du Cerf
© 1991 by Novalis, Université Saint-Paul, Ottawa
and Editions du Cerf, Paris

Translation © John Bowden and Margaret Lydamore 1993

Illustrations
p. 2, Christ in Judgment, fresco in the Cathedral of Anagni (Scala Fine
Arts); p. 12, Sacking of Jerusalem, bas-relief on the Arch of Titus, Rome
(Archivi Alinari); p. 24, the Dragon giving his Power to the Beast,
miniature by Facundus illustrating Beatus' Commentary on the
Apocalypse, Biblioteca Nacional, Madrid (folio 191 verso); p. 42, the
Fourth Trumpet, miniature from the Apocalypse of Saint-Sever, Biblio-
thèque Nationale, Paris (Latin manuscript 8878, folio 8); p. 48, Saint
John and the Angel, miniature from the Apocalypse of Saint-Victor,
Bibliothèque Nationale, Paris (Latin manuscript 14410); p. 58, the First
Rider, thirteenth-century miniature, Bibliothèque Municipale de
Cambrai (manuscript 422, folio 18 verso); p. 68, Letters to the Churches
in Ephesus and in Pergamum, miniatures by Facundus illustrating
Beatus' Commentary on the Apocalypse, Biblioteca Nacional, Madrid
(folios 78 recto and 87 verso); p. 78, Vision of the Mystical Lamb,
miniature by Facundus illustrating Beatus' Commentary on the
Apocalypse, Biblioteca Nacional, Madrid (folio 117 verso); p. 88, the
Multitude of 144,000, miniature from the Apocalypse of Saint-Sever,
Bibliothèque Nationale, Paris (Latin manuscript 8878, folio 6); p. 98, the
Woman and the Dragon, thirteenth-century miniature, Bibliothèque
Municipale de Cambrai (manuscript 422, folio 47 recto); p. 106, the New
Jerusalem, eleventh-century miniature, Bibliothèque Municipale de
Cambrai (manuscript 386, folio 41 recto).
Drawings on pages 11, 22, 30, 54, 64, 81, 93, 101, 112
by Malgosia Chelkowska.

Library of Congress Cataloging-in-Publication Data
Prévost, Jean-Pierre.
[Pour lire l'Apocalypse. English]
How to read the Apocalypse / Jean-Pierre Prévost:
[translated by John Bowden and Margaret Lydamore from the French]
p.     cm.
Includes bibliographical references.
ISBN 0–8245–1280–4 (pbk.)
1.  Bible.  N.T.  Revelation--Criticism, Interpretation, etc.
1.  Title.
BS2825.2.P72513   1993                                93–16880
228' . 06--dc20                                       CIP

Printed in Great Britain

# Contents

**Introduction**     vii

**Part One:  Five Keys to Reading**

  1. Discovering the Christ of the Apocalypse     1
  2. Reading Prophecy for the Present     13
  3. The Apocalypse in Figures and Colours: Learning the Symbols     25
  4. Entering into the World of the Apocalypses     43
  5. The Apocalypse is Good News!     59

**Part Two:  Studying Texts**

  6. Hear what the Spirit says to the Churches . . . (Apocalypse 2–3)     69
  7. 'The Lamb Standing as Though it had been Slain'
       or the True Face of God (Apocalypse 4–5)     79
  8. From Judgment to Salvation (Apocalypse 6–7)     89
  9. The Battle of the Dragon with the Woman (Apocalypse 12)     99
 10. From the 'End of the World' to a New Creation
       (Apocalypse 21–22)     107

**The Last Word**     114

**For Further Reading**     117

## List of Boxes

The Apocalypse and the End of the World in *The Name of the Rose*   viii
Liturgical Acclamations of Christ in the Apocalypse   5
John of the Apocalypse   14
The Prophets at Risk from the Calendar   16
Five Dates to Remember for Understanding the Apocalypse   18
The Two Problems of the Hour   20
The Apocalypse, A War Book   23
Talking of 'Numbers'   29
Can You Interpret the Number of Christ?   40
What is Apocalyptic?   44
The Biblical Roots of Apocalyptic   52
The Seven Beatitudes in the Apocalypse   60
Re-experiencing the Exodus   82
The Enigma of the First Rider   94
Apocalypse 7.9–17 and the Feast of Tabernacles   96
The Antichrist – an Apocalyptic Figure?   102
How to Study the Rest of the Apocalypse   116

## List of Diagrams

The Titles of Christ   6
The Symbolism of Colours   28
The Symbolism of Numbers   33
Numbers and Letters – Greek Style   37
To Help You Get Your Bearings   45
Prophets – Apocalypse   65
Apocalypse 2–3   70
The Dynamics of Judgment and Salvation in Apocalypse 6–22   91
Apocalypse 12–20   104
From Lamentations to Glorification in Apocalypse 17 and 21–22   110

# INTRODUCTION

In the history of Christian interpretation, few biblical books can claim such unique and complex fortunes as the Apocalypse of John. Together with the Psalms and the Gospel of John, it is clearly one of the most frequently used and commented-on books in the Bible. But it is also amongst the most controversial books and one of those which have given rise to the most varied interpretations. With the Song of Songs and Ecclesiastes, it is recognized as one of the most enigmatic, posing difficulties to interpreters which are almost insurmountable. In other words, it has enjoyed both favour and disfavour with the Christian public.

The main points of the debate have been made clear since the first centuries of the Christian era, with fundamentalist readings, augmented by millenarian speculations from the Ebionite and Montanist sects, and more finely shaded interpretations of a symbolic type from Origen and Augustine. From these first centuries to the present day, right through the Middle Ages and the Reformation, the debate has never stopped, and if it has prompted a great variety of literary and artistic works, it has always raised the same basic questions. Must we read the Apocalypse of John as a writing from the past, a witness to an age and events which are irretrievably gone? Or must we read it as an anticipation of the future, a future which has still to take shape, but which *could* be quite close?

It is surely a surprise to come upon the word apocalypse in the title of a peculiar and depressing film made by Francis Coppola in 1979, *Apocalypse Now?* Granted, the film wasn't any great success, either on the big screen or afterwards on television. And Francis Coppola doesn't seem to be able to give a reason for the title. But it's easy to work out. It expresses the sense of weariness, impotence and failure felt by a whole generation of Americans following the withdrawal of American forces from Vietnam. The failure of the Vietnam war became in some ways a kind of symbol indicative of the end of the world. At the same time, this film of excess and violence suggests a catastrophic interpretation of the word apocalypse, and probably also of the biblical book from which it was taken.

The huge success of a novel such as *The Name of the Rose* by the Italian Umberto Eco, which is as passionate as it is difficult, also testifies to the intensity of the 'apocalyptic' preoccupations of our generation. It

# The Apocalypse and the End of the World in *The Name of the Rose*

Umberto Eco's novel can be read at different levels. For a simple enjoyment of words, as a detective story, to apply its parable to the present day, for the history of the orders and religious monasteries in the Middle Ages, for its references to Aristotle, and so on. It has more than its fair share of theology; and speculations on the cheerfulness or severity of the Christ of the Gospels, references to the Apocalypse and the themes of the end of the world and the Antichrist, have quite an important place in it. Here is an attempt to trace the apocalyptic thread in this novel.

p. 15: Adso conjures up 'the disaster of an aging world' and describes its decadence.

p. 24: William mentions that the universe 'speaks of the ultimate things'.

p. 36: The abbot speaks of the warnings of Providence that 'the end of the world is approaching', that there will be a definitive 'millennium' and 'the triumph, however brief, of the foul beast that is the Antichrist'.

p. 62: Ubertino 'prophesies' and, referring to the teaching of Joachim of Fiore, identifies the two Antichrists. He alludes to the beast with seven heads and ten horns, cites the name of Apollyon and sees him as Benedict XI, 'the beast that rises up from the earth': 'But the number of the beast, if you read the name in Greek letters, is Benedict!'

p. 83: Jorge, the librarian, enlightens Adso on one of his namesakes, who was the author of a book entitled *Libellus de Antechristo*, and adds his personal commentary: 'The ways of the Antichrist are slow and tortuous. He arrives when we do not expect him: not because the calculation suggested by the apostle was mistaken, but because we have not learned the art.'

pp. 157–9: The conversation between William and the aged Alinardo is about the Beast. Alinardo is convinced that this is going to come soon, since, he says, 'the millennium is past' (158). To William's objections that it has already been past for three hundred years (the year 1000), the old man replies that it has to be calculated 'from the Donation of Constantine' (158).

pp. 169–74: William and Adso penetrate the labyrinth. They find themselves in a heptagonal room; above one of the archways, a big scroll, painted on the wall, bore the words '*Apocalypsis Jesu Christi*' (169). They see other scrolls and other inscriptions, all in Latin: these are verses from the Apocalypse, and only by deciphering these verses (above all 4.4, 'the twenty-four elders upon their seats') are they able to find their way through the labyrinth and gain access to the mysterious library (see also 318).

pp. 397–405: At compline on the fifth day, Jorge delivers a fiery sermon on the Antichrist: he quotes the severe warning from Apocalypse 22.18–19. Alluding to the pride which has sown disorder in the monastery, he attributes this to the Antichrist, 'the foul beast', but he takes care to add: '. . . I am not so ingenuous; I will not single out one man for you. The Antichrist, when he comes, comes in all and for all, and each is a part of him' (401).

p. 501: at the very end, Adso relates his return 'many years later' to the site of the ruined abbey and cannot help quoting Apocalypse 18: '*Est ubi gloria nunc Babylonia?* – Babylon, where has your glory gone?' So the abbey was Babylon, the woman in the service of the Beast!

(Quotations from Umberto Eco, *The Name of the Rose*, Secker and Warburg and Harcourt, Brace Jovanovich 1983) has been translated into twenty-seven languages and to date has sold more than ten million copies. It, too, has been brought to the screen, by the director Jean-Jacques Annaud in 1986. If the enormous success of the novel cannot just be attributed to interest in the Apocalypse, this aspect is no less crucial to the organization of the book (see the box on page viii): the mysterious library of the monastery is divided up according to the verses of the Apocalypse; speculations on the identity of the Antichrist and the imminent ending of the world play a key part; and finally the perpetrator of the series of murders, in a last sermon before the final assault, delivers a solemn address on the Antichrist. Admittedly, the action is placed fictitiously in the Middle Ages, but one cannot fail to see here a parable of the present-day world, beset with the same preoccupations.

These two star productions aren't isolated cases. Quite the contrary. They are part of a vast apocalyptic revival, already well under way at the beginning of the 1970s and which goes on intensifying as the day of reckoning represented by the year 2000, deemed by a great many to be crucial, even fateful, comes ever nearer. In fact for the last twenty years the apocalyptic vein has enjoyed a quite remarkable success, as much at the level of fiction as at the level of religious and even esoteric thought.

For the 1970s, it is enough to recall the incomparable success of the short book by Hal Lindsey, *The Late Great Planet Earth*, which appeared precisely in 1970 and proved to be the religious best-seller of the decade, with more than fifteen million copies sold. This book was to become the absolute spiritual guide of fundamentalist readers of biblical prophecy, and more specifically of the Apocalypse of John. One could say that Lindsey founded a school, so numerous were the 'preachers', Catholic as well as Protestant, who took up or copied, or refined his argument to discern in biblical prophecy, and more especially in the Apocalypse of John, a description of the final events which must take place before long. The original publishers of Lindsey's book had taken the trouble to print above the title: *The 1980s – Countdown to Armageddon*.

The theme spread wider with the 1980s. Besides novels, like *The Name of the Rose* and Morris West's *The Clowns of God* (1982), disaster movies also proliferated, and others than *Apocalypse Now?* had apocalyptic titles. They still continue.

Of all the talk about the end of things, that concerned with the threat of a nuclear war has undoubtedly been the most credible or the most probable. In the autumn of 1983, President Reagan was confiding to an Israeli official: 'I wonder if we aren't the generation which will see the fulfilment of the portents of Armageddon' (*Chicago Sun-Times*, 29 October 1983). A few months later, in his New Year message, one of the great world leaders, Pope John-Paul II, invited Washington and Moscow to continue and speed up negotiations, calling attention to the terrible threats which weigh upon humankind: 'The threat of nuclear disaster and the scourge of famine appear terrifyingly on the horizon, like the fatal horsemen of the Apocalypse.' In spite of the new climate of *détente* which prevails today between East and West, the never-ending conflicts of the Near East and the Persian Gulf do not give us much relief from the concept of a total holocaust, such as the one illustrated by a film like *The Day After* (1983).

The preoccupations of ecologists, too, have assumed a faint tinge of apocalyptic. Here, again, awareness came with the oil crisis, an awareness which consisted first of all in a realization of our misuse of resources and the evil inflicted by human beings on their environment. It was the awakening, too, of an old dream of a return to a lost Paradise and of a greater communion with nature. In that sense, the ecology movement brings together two great strands of the apocalyptic tradition: first, the present-day world is evil because of irresponsible and depraved human intervention; and secondly, a break with this world is sought in the expectation of the coming of a new world which will re-establish the equilibrium we had at the very beginning.

It is in this context of deep anxiety that we are invited to re-read the Apocalypse today. We should approach it with a bias in its favour and try to understand all that there is to be understood, but without reading into it what is not there. Who could possibly solve all the difficulties and enigmas of this book? Still, the fact remains that this is a book which is not only coherent but important, and has value for us today. In this case more than in any other, in view of the seriousness of the questions raised by the text and the complexity of the symbols which are used, it is appropriate to proceed methodically and to equip ourselves with keys to reading which will allow us to unlock a book which some people think is irrevocably sealed.

The aim of this study, therefore, is to be an introduction to reading the Apocalypse of John. Each of the keys suggested here is relevant to the book as a whole. They invite a reconsideration of the whole text in such a way as to avoid being open to manipulation from views based solely on isolated passages, and enigmatic ones at that. Each of these keys represents the broad consensus of a number of experts, but it is the force of the text that supports their use. Readers will be able to judge them by the light they shed on the biblical text. I remain deeply convinced that the Apocalypse must be understood through the Apocalypse, and that only repeated reading of the whole text will reveal the power and coherence of its message.

Besides, John's work is a magnificently constructed one, and it has seemed important to me to study in more detail some of the features which support the general architecture of the book. Hence the second part: a study of texts which allows readers a better understanding of individual details of the work, by putting them in perspective and pointing to the links which the author has made between the different sections of his work.

A series of boxes and diagrams summarize particular problems or give swift and succinct information on this and that aspect of the Apocalypse. They are listed on page vi.

# PART ONE

# FIVE KEYS TO READING

## 1

# Discovering the Christ of the Apocalypse

A large number of Christian men and women have chosen to have nothing to do with the Apocalypse, on the grounds that the book is a very difficult one and moreover too loaded with symbolism and an Old Testament mentality. At its most extreme, this approach would see the Apocalypse as a Jewish apocalypse, lightly revised and Christianized, but has difficulties in seeing it as a book that is really and profoundly Christian. The violence of the language, the calls for divine vengeance and the heaping up of proclamations of disaster do not fit well, people say, with the message of Jesus and the New Testament, which is essentially good news. What is the point of reading this kind of work? Present reality is tormenting and depressing enough as it is.

By contrast, others devour this book with an insatiable appetite, but unfortunately for the wrong reasons. They want to know more about the Beast and the ravages which it is supposed to perpetrate in the world. To look at popular publications of recent years, the Beast of the Apocalypse seems to be more popular than the Lamb.

The irony of fate has thus brought it about that

a book which is not only Christian but clearly and deeply christological has been distorted by a disproportionate interest in the Beast. Although the latter has a part to play in the battle evoked by the Apocalypse, it is far from being the central figure in the book. We have to look for that elsewhere. It is amazing that people can read this book without seeing who upholds the whole structure. This central figure is Christ, dead and risen.

Of the five keys for reading the Apocalypse suggested here, this first key, which consists in bringing together all that it says about Christ, is certainly the most important and the most fertile. It alone demystifies alarmist readings of the Apocalypse which focus on catastrophe. We must read the Apocalypse for good reasons. If we read it to solve the enigma of the Beast, with its seven heads and ten horns, or to set out the scenario of the Battle of Armageddon, we shall be fatally deceived. But if we read it to discover something about Jesus Christ, we shall be served royally! Do it for that reason alone, to reveal the riches of the person of Christ and the significance of the events of his death and resurrection for the future of the world, and the audacious and

undoubtedly arduous undertaking which led to the writing of the Apocalypse will have been amply justified.

The 'centrality' of Christ in the Apocalypse is the result of the following four elements: 1. the title (1.1), which directs us both to the object and the source of the book, Jesus Christ; 2. a certain number of visions situated at strategic points in the narrative (prologue and epilogue; chapters 1 and 22; chapters 4, 5 and 12); 3. the liturgical acclamations which express the living faith of a community (1.4–7; 5.9–10, 12, 13; 7.10; 11.15; 19.6–7); 4. and finally, scattered throughout the book, a collection unrivalled in the whole of the New Testament of christological titles, some of them traditional and some of them peculiar to John, author of the Apocalypse.

## A 'revelatory' title

As in the case of all ancient writings, the 'headings' of the biblical books are especially important for the understanding of the genre and the content of the book which they introduce. That of the Apocalypse could not be more 'revelatory'. The translation of the first four words of the Greek text reads as follows: 'The revelation of Jesus Christ' (1.1). This could have two meanings: a revelation experienced by Jesus Christ (in which case he is the source or agent of it); or a revelation about Jesus Christ (in which case he is the object of it). Either is grammatically possible, and it is usually the first which is favoured by commentators. But it seems advisable sometimes to me to prefer the second because of all the strands in the book which set out this 'relevation of Jesus' in the most complete way.

## The visions which give us our bearings

The author is able in this way to reawaken the hope of his brothers and sisters 'under trial' by pointing them resolutely to the figure of Christ, dead and risen again.

The whole of his book is framed by this figure, who appears in all his power and who generates an infinite hope. In fact, the opening vision (1.9–20) is centred upon this mysterious figure, who stands out 'as a Son of Man' (1.13), and presents himself as 'the living one; I died, and behold I am alive for evermore, and I have the keys of Death and Hades' (1.18); in other words, in the form of the Risen One, fit to communicate his power of life and resurrection.

In the same way, and like an echo, the final vision (22.12–20) takes us back to the same figure, Alpha and Omega, who invites believers to enter fully into his paschal mystery: 'I am the Alpha and the Omega, the first and the last, the beginning and the end. Blessed are those who wash their robes, that they may have the right to the tree of life and that they may enter the city by the gates' (22.13, 14). He is the One whose coming 'the Spirit and the Bride' pray for with a heavenly impatience: 'Come! . . . Amen, come, Lord Jesus' (22.17, 20).

It is no coincidence that the book begins and ends with a vision of Christ. From the first vision derives the whole understanding of history presented throughout the book, and from the final vision is born the most fervent hope which is to inspire Christians as they wait for the return of Christ. If everything begins from the resurrection of Christ, it all moves forward under the inspiration of the hope for his return.

Furthermore, since the Apocalypse consists of two major parts (4–11 and 12–22), it is important to note the strategic importance of the two visions which have as their object first the Lamb and secondly the male child. Chapter 4 from the start puts us in the heavenly world, in the presence of the Living One, sitting on the throne. But we immediately encounter a great dramatic tension which culminates in chapter 5, where John deplores the fact that no one can open the sealed book. Now the Lamb holds this power and will effectively open the seals. Here, too, we can talk of the central role of Christ, first of all retrospectively, since he has power to explain the book, i.e. the Old Testament, and then prospectively: he is the one who unveils the imminent unfolding of history with the opening of the seven seals.

The position of the second vision is perhaps less expected. It is interesting to note that in a part which attaches so much importance to the Beast (this will be found above all in chapters 12–22) and which is devoted to a virulent charge against the imperial Roman power, everything is set under the sign of a vision of the dead Christ (his 'birth', 12.5) and the risen Christ (his being 'caught up' to heaven, 12.6). In this part neither the Dragon nor the Beast have the first or the last word. It is still Christ dead and risen who is the foundation for the hope of Christians and who struggles with the Beast and his supporters.

## The Christ professed in faith

There is no doubt about the liturgical character of the Apocalypse. It is nothing new for a religion which has emerged from Jewish monotheism to venerate and celebrate the holy and all-powerful God. But it is a new fact, which became increasingly prominent in the primitive church, for him to be associated with Christ. Such a new development is already well under way in the Apocalypse.

It is quite clear that there is a community or, as some would say, a school, behind the whole of the Apocalypse. But this draws primarily on liturgical formulae which have been developed by and for community use. In other words, they bear witness to a faith shared by the community, and not to a point of view which is strictly personal to John. It is worth discussing the selection of passages contained in the box entitled 'The Liturgical Acclamations of Christ in the Apocalypse' (page 4), which results in a series (another series!) of seven . . . Was there a concern to make this a condensed catechism which would prove exhaustive? At any rate, an examination of these liturgical acclamations will shed much light on the role of Christ in the Apocalypse.

The first of these professions of faith comes at the end of a trinitarian formula: 'Grace to you and peace from "He is, He was and He is coming", and from the seven spirits who are before his throne, and from Jesus Christ the faithful witness, the first-born of the dead, and the ruler of kings on earth. To him who loves us and has freed us from our sins by his blood and made us a kingdom of priests, to his God and Father, to him be glory and dominion for ever and ever. Amen. Behold, he is coming with the clouds; every eye will see him, everyone who pierced him and all tribes of the earth will wail on account of him. Even so. Amen' (1.4–7). Everything in this acclamation is aimed at bringing out the importance of Christ. The Spirit is mentioned here before Christ to leave the way free for an expansion of the christological formula. The saving action of Christ is the feature which is developed most fully, and the acclamation is punctuated by a two-fold 'Amen'. The emphasis is put on the death-resurrection, but the last part of the acclamation also introduces the theme of Christ's coming, of his return.

In chapter 5 the heavenly liturgy, which has already proclaimed the greatness and holiness of the Living One, essentially acknowledges the same attributes in the Lamb, standing as though it had been slain: power and glory, and so on, and celebrates him as it celebrates God, with 'honour' and 'praise'. Twice out of three times in this chapter the foundation of such worship is directly linked to the death of the Lamb: 'for you were slain', and 'worthy is the Lamb who was slain . . .' (vv. 9, 12). The mention of the dignity of the Lamb and his royal attributes aims to bring out the fullness of life and power held by the Risen Christ.

The acclamation of 7.10, 'Salvation belongs to our God who sits upon the throne, and to the Lamb,' is doubly interesting. First, it comes almost at the end of the first series of seals (since the seventh coincides with the first trumpet) and underlines the saving dimension of the Lamb's work. Secondly, it is given a clearly universalist connotation by the fact that it is put on the lips of 'a great multitude which no man could number from all tribes and peoples and tongues'. Here is the Christ acclaimed by the nations.

The acclamation in chapter 11 is no less

# Liturgical Acclamations of Christ in the Apocalypse

**1.4–7**

'Grace to you and peace from "He is, He was and He is coming", and from the seven spirits who are before his throne, and from Jesus Christ the faithful witness, the First-born of the dead, and the Ruler of kings on earth. To him who loves us and has freed us from our sins by his blood and made us a kingdom of priests, to his God and Father, to him be glory and dominion for ever and ever. Amen. Behold, he is coming with the clouds; every eye will see him, everyone who pierced him and all tribes of the earth will wail on account of him. Even so. Amen.'

**5.9–10**

'You are worthy to take the scroll and to open its seals, for you were slain and by your blood you ransomed men for God from every tribe and tongue and people and nation, and made them a kingdom of priests to our God, and they shall reign on earth.'

**5.12**

'Worthy is the Lamb who was slain, to receive power and wealth and wisdom and might and honour and glory and blessing!'

**5.13**

'To him who sits upon the throne and to the Lamb be blessing and honour and glory and might for ever and ever!'

**7.10**

'Salvation belongs to our God who sits upon the throne, and to the Lamb!'

**11.15**

'The kingdom of the world has become the kingdom of our Lord and of his Christ, and he shall reign for ever and ever.'

**19.6–7**

'Hallelujah! For the Lord our God the Almighty reigns. Let us rejoice and exult and give him the glory, for the marriage of the Lamb has come, and his bride has made herself ready.'

interesting. This time we have reached not only the seventh trumpet but the end of the first major section. All that has gone before abounds in symbols from the Old Testament, and the few verses which follow will evoke the most important elements of the first covenant: the revelation on Sinai, the ark and the temple. By putting the acclamation 'The kingdom of the world has become the kingdom of our Lord and of his Christ, and he shall reign for ever and ever' here,

| The Titles of Christ (see page 8) | |
|---|---|
| Reference | Title |
| 1.1, 2, 5, 9; 12.17; 14.12; 17.6; 19.10; 20.4; 22.16, 20, 21 | Jesus |
| 1.1, 2, 5; 11.15; 12.10; 20.4, 6 | Christ |
| 1.5 | the faithful witness |
| 1.5 | the First-born of the dead |
| 1.5 | the Ruler of kings on earth |
| 1.5 | who loves us and has freed us from our sins by his blood |
| 1.6 | who has made us a kingdom of priests, to his God and Father |
| 1.13; 14.14 | a Son of man |
| 1.17; 2.8; 22.13 | the First and the Last |
| 1.18 | the Living one; I died, and behold I am alive for evermore, and I have the keys of death and Hades |
| 2.1; 3.1 | who holds the seven stars |
| 2.1 | who walks among the seven golden lampstands |
| 2.8 | who died and came to life |
| 2.12 | who has the sharp two-edged sword |
| 2.18 | The words of the Son of God |
| 2.18 | (The words of the Son of God), who has eyes like a flame of fire and whose feet are like burnished bronze |
| 2.23 | I am he who searches mind and heart |

the author has killed two birds with one stone. First, he relates Christ to the Old Testament: it is in him that the hope of the first covenant is fulfilled. And secondly, in a more subtle but radical way he anticipates the second part: while this second part will give a full description of the Beast's claims to power, the author states quite bluntly that the one who is in charge of the world is not the Roman emperor, but 'our Lord', and 'his Christ'.

| | |
|---|---|
| 3.1 | The words of him who has the seven spirits of God and the seven stars |
| 3.7 | The words of the Holy One |
| 3.7; 19.11 | the True One |
| 3.7 | who has the key of David |
| 3.14 | The words of the Amen, the faithful and true witness |
| 3.14 | the beginning of God's creation |
| 5.5 | the Lion of the tribe of Judah |
| 5.5; 22.16 | the Root of David |
| 5.6, 8, 12, 13; 6.1, 16; 7.9, 10, 14, 17; 12.11; 13.8; 14.1, 4, 10; 15.3; 17.14; 19.7, 9; 21.9, 14, 22, 23, 27; 22.1, 3 | the Lamb |
| 5.6, 12; 13.8 | a Lamb, as though it had been slain |
| 11.8 | their Lord |
| 12.5 | a male child, one who is to rule all the nations with a rod of iron |
| 19.13 | the Word of God |
| 19.16 | King of kings and Lord of lords |
| 21.6; 22.13 | I am the Alpha and the Omega, the First and the Last |
| 22.16 | the bright morning Star |

Finally, the last acclamation (19.6–7) is beyond doubt the most festive. In its invitations to rejoice it is a vivid contrast with the funeral lament on Babylon (ch. 18): 'Hallelujah! . . . Let us rejoice and exult and give God the glory . . .' The 'let us' includes the great multitude. Nor are the readers of the Apocalypse to be left out; they, too, are invited to rejoice at the victory of the Lamb over the Beast. This last acclamation introduces the theme of 'the marriage of the Lamb' and already celebrates the union of the bride with the Lamb.

## The titles of Christ: an unparalleled collection

So far in this chapter, leaving aside the explanation of the title of the Apocalypse, we have been considering longer passages: whole pericopes or verses. Now we need to look at much shorter and more numerous references, known as christological titles. The classical names Jesus and the Christ appear first, as is their due. But the author excels in commenting on them or replacing them with symbolic names or expressions which bring out different aspects of the identity and activity of Christ. The box on the previous page contains a complete list of these titles, with their references. It is easy to see how wide is the range of the titles used by John and to note how they are distributed right through the chapters of the book (in fact it is only in chapter 4 and the sequence of seven trumpets in chapters 8, 9 and 10 that none of them are to be found).

## A dazzling Christ

The list is all the more impressive, not only for the quality but also for the quantity of the images of Christ which it projects. Note the important concentration of christological titles in the first three chapters (for example, in the addresses to each of the seven churches the author succeeds in presenting Christ with the help of several new titles). So from the start he is able to focus our attention on the one who gives meaning to all human history, including that which unfolds in the confrontation with the Beast.

Better still, the Apocalypse commends itself by the power of its concentration on Jesus Christ: not just any Jesus, with imprecise or neutral features, but a radiant and resplendent Jesus Christ. In fact, unlike the Gospels, the christology of which is steeped in the paschal experience but which pay considerable attention to the earthly Jesus and his public ministry, the Apocalypse of John is uniquely devoted to the decisive event of the life of Jesus, his death and resurrection. This is the great originality of the Apocalypse: the ability to work out the implications of the death and resurrection of Jesus for the present world. We should note the degree to which John was able to hold together the two inseparable facets of this unique mystery (Christ presents himself as 'the Living One', but not without recalling that he '(was) dead' and the victorious Lamb appears as though 'slain'). By retaining the two facets of the mystery, John never leaves any doubt about the outcome of this event: it is the pole of the resurrection which illuminates the death of the crucified Lord (a past event) as much as the present and the future of believers (the struggle with the Beast and the final fate of humanity, represented here by the new Jerusalem). In the Apocalypse of John it is the resurrection of Christ which illuminates the whole work; one could not find a more dazzling, a more blazing christology. John is the indefatigable interpreter and witness of a Christ who had vanquished death and is the first fruit of a new world. The Christ of John and the Apocalypse is the Christ in glory represented on so many Christian icons and mosaics and given as inspiration to the prayer of Christians.

In this immense fresco in honour of the Risen Christ, four features in particular stand out: the Christ appears above all as the Lamb, the Living One, the Lord and King, and He who is to come.

## The Lamb

Appearing for the first time in chapter 5, the figure of the Lamb certainly stands out as *the* title for Christ in the Apocalypse. Here John uses a term which is in fact unknown to the rest of the New Testament, the Greek *arnion* (which occurs 29 times). Elsewhere the New Testament uses a synonymous term (*amnos*) four times (John 1.19, 36; Acts 8.32 quoting Isa. 53.7; I Peter 1.19) to denote the Christ. The symbolism is essentially the same, but the disproportionate frequency of usage obliges us to give priority to the text of the Apocalypse to establish the christological sense of the term.

Here John has fused a number of traditions from the Old Testament in the way that he does so well. First of all there is the tradition of the paschal lamb which in the Old Testament is associated with *the* saving event, the Exodus. As a later box will indicate (see page 82), the Exodus theme is omnipresent in the Apocalypse and is confirmed and reinforced by the presentation of Christ the Lamb, who takes over from the paschal lamb (Ex. 12.3–6): it is he who delivers the new people of God by his blood. Sacrificed like the lamb of the first passover, in his resurrection Christ goes before a people whom he will lead towards the promised land of a definitive and unhindered freedom.

Again on the basis of the Exodus, John also evokes the Servant Songs, particularly Isaiah 52–53. We should not forget that these songs do not go back to the classical prophet of the eighth century but to the period of the return from exile, which a new prophet interprets in terms of the new Exodus: the Servant 'like a lamb that is led to the slaughter' (53.7) gives his life for the salvation of all. Brought down and almost overwhelmed by suffering, 'he shall see the fruit of the travail of his soul and be satisfied', and will then be able to justify 'many' (53.11). Who is this mysterious servant of the text of Isaiah? The prophet himself? The community? The Messiah? It is difficult to decide. One thing is certain: his destiny will determine the fate of Jerusalem (ch. 54). So this is a text which would provide an ideal framework for John's reflection, in his purpose to demonstrate the saving significance of Christ for the multitudes and his deep concern for the new Jerusalem. The Lamb is synonymous with victory, so we should not be surprised to read of him 'standing on Mount Zion' (14.1). For he is the one charged with healing Jerusalem and restoring all its splendour, to make the Jerusalem of the final salvation, to which all the nations are invited: 'And the city has no need of sun or moon to shine upon it, for the glory of God is its light, and its lamp is the Lamb. By its light shall the nations walk and the kings of the earth shall bring their glory into it, and its gates shall never be shut by day – and there shall be no night there; they shall bring into it the glory and the honour of the nations' (21.23–26).

Finally, we should remember that in a book in which fantastic animals come to represent the divine and the terrestrial worlds in turn, particular attention is paid to two of them. The first is humble and inoffensive: the Lamb once slain. The other makes a monstrous impact and attacks all living beings: it is the Beast. The latter ends up by drawing blood in its claim to universal domination. But its power is usurped and can only be provisional. The Beast exists, unfortunately, but in a time and space which are clearly demarcated. As for the Lamb, he does not seek his own glory and does not fear to give up his life out of love, as a ransom for all. The Apocalypse is a great book of hope, because it celebrates the victory of the Lamb over the Beast, the victory of life over death, the victory of love over hatred and violence: 'Worthy is the Lamb who was slain . . .' (7.12).

## The Living One

The whole Bible, including the Apocalypse (4.9–10), loves to see God as the Living One *par excellence*. John applies this title in an absolute form to the Risen Christ: '. . . I am the Living One; I died, and behold I am alive for evermore, and I have the keys of Death and Hades' (1.17–18). Only one other text in the New Testament dared to use this title before John, again in a paschal context: 'Why do you seek the Living One among the dead? He is not here, he is risen'

(Luke 24.5–6). John deepened this way of looking at Christ: throughout his book he multiplies references to life: possessed in fullness by the Risen Christ, this life is offered to believers and shared by those who have been willing to die with and for Christ. But with the vocabulary of life John sends us back once more to the unique mystery of the death and resurrection of Christ, which he does not consider a distant event of the past but as the finest manifestation of life and the surest of promises: 'To him who conquers I will grant to eat of the tree of life, which is in the paradise of God' (2.7).

## The Lord and King

John attaches numerous attributes to Christ. Among them it is easy to see the important part assigned to imagery of a royal kind: honour, power, dignity, etc. Twice Christ is hailed as 'Lord of lords and king of kings' (17.14, 19.16), and the first part of the book ends on an acclamation which recognizes the definitive establishment of the 'kingdom of Christ': 'The kingdom of the world has become the kingdom of our Lord and of his Christ, and he shall reign for ever and ever' (11.15). Such a designation for Christ stands out all the more when the second half unveils to us the monstrous efforts of the Beast to impose its domination on all the world. For John, this is an abusive and senseless enterprise, in direct contradiction to the conviction of Christians, for whom there can be only one Lord: the Risen Christ.

If John has taken care in this way to relativize the claims of the Beast, we should not suppose that the royal imagery is limited to the last great section of the Apocalypse. It is already very much present in the first chapters, where it is to be found as a development of the great messianic expectations as expressed by the prophets and the psalms or even by the traditions about the Exodus:

Christ is the 'ruler of kings on earth' (1.5: cf. Ps. 89.28);

'He has made us a kingdom of priests (1.6 cf. Ex. 19.6);

In the inaugural vision he appears 'clothed with a long robe and with a golden girdle round his breast': this is the symbol of royal dignity (1.13; cf. I Macc. 10.89; 11.58, where a 'golden buckle' is given to the kinsmen of kings);

Finally, he is the one who fulfils the great messianic promise made to David: indeed he is of the line of David (3.7; 5.5; 22.16) and sits on the royal throne (3.21; 5.65; 7.17; 22.3): cf. II Sam. 7 and Ps. 89.

Once more, John bases himself on an element which is not unknown in the New Testament but which he develops more than any other author: the royal dignity of Christ, attained through his resurrection, which reduces to nothing the efforts of the Beast in its struggle to usurp equal dignity.

## He who is coming

The christology of the Apocalypse is essentially dynamic and directed towards the future. As elsewhere, it is given an eschatological colouring. In other words, the Christ of the Apocalypse does not come from the past but from the future: 'Behold, he is coming with the clouds, and every eye will see him . . .' (1.7). In a revolutionary and passionate book written in Italian and translated into English as *The Apocalypse: The Perennial Revelation of Jesus Christ*, the scholar E. Corsini makes an entirely christological reading of the Apocalypse. The whole of his commentary is refreshing and remarkably coherent. But in interpreting the texts as speaking only of the first and not of the second coming of Christ, he does not seem to do justice to those texts, frequent as they are, which speak of the coming of Christ 'soon': 'I will come to you soon' (2.16; cf. 2.5; 3.11, 20).

Granted, it will always be possible to go on discussing the length of the delay implied by this 'soon' (the apocalyptists have a very lively sense of urgency, and in a way they see everything as being 'soon'). But the insistent reprise of this theme at the end of the book, 'Behold, I am coming soon' (22.12; cf. also v. 7), projects us unfailingly towards the future. Indeed it is the expectation of this return which upholds all the hope of the church: 'The Spirit and the Bride say, "Come!"' (22.17). Before the author's final salutation, the last words of the community are a vibrant appeal addressed to the Christ who is to come: 'Amen, come Lord Jesus!' (22.20).

## In conclusion

Other titles would be worth studying: Man of Man, Alpha and Omega, Firstborn from among the dead, Faithful Witness, and so on. The christology of the Apocalypse is especially fruitful. If anyone asks 'Why read the Apocalypse?', the unhesitating answer must be, 'To know Christ better'. He alone holds the key to the book, and any interpretation which leaves him out can only go in quite the wrong direction. By contrast, in choosing to enter the Apocalypse with the christological key, we find everything in its proper light and in perspective.

# 2

# Reading Prophecy
# for the Present

## Prophecies and prophecy

Struck by amazing similarities between our age and the phenomena which are described in the Apocalypse of John, a large number of writings or popular discussions avidly scrutinize the last book of the Bible and call on its witness to fill out their own vision of an imminent end of the world. They say that our generation was envisaged by the writer on Patmos, who was divinely instructed in the secrets of the future. So they read the prophecy in terms of the future. Prophecy is thus, as in current usage, equivalent to prediction of the future: the prophets become soothsayers. So we should not be surprised to see such different figures as Ezekiel, Daniel and John for the biblical period and St Malachias (twelfth century), Nostradamus (sixteenth century) and Edgar Cayce (twentieth century), to mention only the soothsayers who receive the greatest attention today, lumped together in what is presented as a remarkable convergence and even unanimity. All are said to have 'prophesied' the end of the world, and we are said to have reached a critical period, in which the greater part of their 'prophecies' will be fulfilled.

One thing is certain: the Apocalypse of John is a prophetic book, the only one which lays explicit claim to this character among the writings of the New Testament and one of those which has drawn most on the teaching of the biblical prophets – mainly Daniel and Ezekiel, along with Third Isaiah. Two main features remind us of the prophetic character of John's book. First, John has taken the trouble to state at both the beginning and end of his account that he means to deliver a prophetic message: 'Blessed is he who reads aloud the words of the prophecy, and blessed are those who hear, and who keep what is written herein' (1.3; cf. 22.7, 10). And in what could be read as a signature he recalls that his message has now taken the form of a complete book, which demands acceptance as a prophetic writing: 'I warn every one who hears the words of the prophecy of this book: if anyone adds to them, God will add to him the plagues described in this book, and if any one takes away from the words of the book of this prophecy, God will take away his share in the tree of life and in the holy city, which are described in this book' (22.18–19). A second feature recalls the classical prophets of the Bible: the inaugural vision (1.9–20) has all the characteristics of the account of the calling and investiture of the prophets as related in the books of the classical prophets of the Old Testament. For John, too, there is vision and audition, the order to write, the feeling of the unworthiness of the visionary and then confirmation of the mission. John is a true prophet, sent by God to call on his people for vigilance and conversion, and to address to them a word of comfort in their trials.

No one should doubt for a moment that the Apocalypse is a prophecy. But how should we understand and interpret the prophecy?

# John of the Apocalypse

The first name of the author of the Apocalypse is well known to us: he is a certain John (1.1, 4, 9: 22.8). But which John? Is this the John to whom the composition of the Fourth Gospel is attributed by tradition? And if so, can we go so far as to say that he is the Galilean, the son of Zebedee, or the anonymous disciple whom the Fourth Gospel calls 'the disciple whom Jesus loved'?

The question is not as simple as it might seem at first sight. This is first because the text of the Apocalypse does not give us any information on the subject, and the question of the identity of the author of the Fourth Gospel is itself a very complex one.

All we can say is that an ancient tradition, based on Justin (c. 160) and Irenaeus of Lyons (c. 180), sees the Apocalypse as the work of 'one of the apostles of Christ' (Justin, *Dialogue with Trypho*, 81). This tradition is by far the most unanimously attested in the Latin church. However, authors like Gaius, Dionysius of Alexandria and Eusebius of Caesarea did not share this view and, following them, the Greek tradition has been much more reticent about apostolic authorship.

From the perspective of the text, the question remains difficult, if not impossible, to resolve: the verbal or thematic parallels and differences between the Apocalypse and the Gospel of John are evaluated in different ways. There are plenty of both. On the one hand one could appeal to an impressive number of verbal or thematic parallels between the Apocalypse and the Gospel of John: witness (both verb and noun), water, living water, manna, conquer, Word, Lamb (the same theme represented by two different words), etc. On the other hand, it is important not to minimize the differences, indeed the divergences: language, style, literary procedures, visions and symbolism, use of numbers, eschatology, etc. So we need to take account of this two-fold reality – important parallels and no less important differences. Hence the almost unanimous position of recent commentators: the John of the Apocalypse is not necessarily the same as the John to whom the Gospel is attributed. But he belongs within the same sphere or to the same school: the Apocalypse is a Johannine writing, too.

All in all, we should note that as in the case of by far the majority of the biblical books, the precise identification of the author is far from being determinative for the interpretation of the book. One could again talk of the author effacing himself for the benefit of the message, and no matter who this author (or authors) may be who took part in producing the Apocalypse, the most fascinating and profitable task is not to seek to create an identity card but to understand his (their?) work in all its dimensions.

## Rediscovering biblical prophecy

Current usage, based on the etymology and, shall we say, on a possible reading of the prophetic texts, has spontaneously connected 'prophecy', 'prophet' and 'prophesy' with an enterprise of anticipating the future. For example, someone who asks about the possible consequences of such and such an event will be told: 'That's difficult to say, I'm not a prophet . . .' Even in the negative, such a retort says a good deal about the power attributed to those who are in fact prophets to foresee and predict the future.

Such a usage is primarily confirmed from etymology. 'Prophecy' and the words related to it are a transcription of a Greek word composed of the preposition *pro* (= before) and the verb *phemi* (= say, speak). Stress on the temporal sense of the preposition leads people to say that prophecy consists in speaking in advance, predicting events which are to take place in the future.

Another confirmation relates to a principle of interpretation and understanding of links between the Old and New Testaments. A certain Christian understanding of the fulfilment of the scriptures, so often mentioned in the New Testament, in fact suggests that the Old Testament prophets saw the Christ in advance and proclaimed him: they are said to have been instructed in advance on the name and origins of the Messiah, on the events surrounding his birth and death, etc.

Matthew 1.22–23 is a classic example. In order to present the mystery of the conception of Jesus 'by the Holy Spirit', Matthew cites the famous Emmanuel oracle: 'All this took place to fulfil what the Lord had spoken by the prophet: "Behold, a virgin shall conceive and bear a son, and his name shall be called Emmanuel."' According to a practice which lasted a long time, it would be necessary to say that the eighth-century prophet pronounced this oracle specifically with Jesus of Nazareth in view, and that he knew that Jesus was to be conceived of a virgin and to bear the name Emmanuel. Now that is not necessary. All that we can say on the basis of the text of Matthew is that Matthew, along with his community, reread the ancient text of Isaiah, which had a more immediate sense, accessible to Isaiah's contemporaries, in the light of the event of Jesus Christ. The whole of the New Testament claims that Jesus fulfils the Old Testament, but that does not make the prophets people who described coming events down to the last detail.

In other words, classical prophecy takes on a new meaning in the person of Jesus, but this meaning is neither the only meaning nor the original one. The biblical studies of our day stress that biblical prophecy is to be read in its original context. To understand Amos or Isaiah, for example, it is necessary above all to understand the problems and issues of the national and political situation of Israel and Judah in the eighth century before Jesus Christ.

## The prophets and the 'shock of the present'

In fact the biblical prophets are far more people of the present than of the future. Current events are the primary substance of biblical prophecy. Amos, Isaiah, Jeremiah and Ezekiel were prophets above all because they could be men of their time, particularly sensitive to the social and religious context and particularly clear-sighted about the challenges with which their people was confronted. They are, according to the attractive image of Isa. 21.11–12, 'watchmen'. Where others have gone to sleep or are complacent about power and what happens in the society and the religion of the time, the prophets are vigilant and can see what so many others refuse to see. The power of their message stems from their roots in the current situation. And what they want to change is not the distant future but the present: that is what interests them.

In this connection it is worth re-reading the headings of the fifteen books devoted to the writing prophets and all the oracles dated with some precision. Nor should we forget that in the Jewish Bible the books which we call 'historical' like the two books of Samuel and Kings are part of the 'prophetic' books, precisely because it is the prophets more than the kings who guide and interpret the history of the people. The reference to history is quite indispensable to a good interpretation of the message of the prophets. We can easily understand that the task of Amos in a time of prosperity, of unjust luxury and a widespread unawareness of the oppression of the poor (in the eighth century) is different from that of a Jeremiah who has to share with the people the tragic ordeal of the exile (at the beginning of the sixth century). The same goes for the prophecy of the Apocalypse: it is necessary to go through history to understand why and how John, the prophet, adopts the position he does.

## What about the future?

Does that mean that the horizon of the prophets is limited to the immediate present, and that they have nothing to say about the future? Certainly not. But we have to keep things in perspective.

Though men of the present, the prophets are also unwavering in hope, and they never cease to dream of a future in which their people will live in conformity with the covenant and be converted for good to the practice of social justice. Certainly the future interests them, but not in just any way. They have a mission to say at what point God is involved in shaping a future of happiness and justice, not only for his people but for the whole of humanity. The number of oracles which begin 'In those days' and 'On that day' or 'Behold, the days are coming' and announce sometimes the judgment and more often still good news of salvation are countless. So the prophets have much to say about the future, but we should note that they are careful not to fix a precise timetable. Furthermore, the last key to reading (the gospel key) will allow us to see the wealth of the panorama offered by the prophets on the subject of the definitive future of the world, without any of them venturing possible dates.

Moreover, a careful reading of all the biblical prophecies contained in the fifteen books can only lead us to the conclusion that the prophetic oracles which relate to a particular date in the future, and which are thus equivalent to predictions, are extremely rare. Unless I am mistaken, in the whole prophetic corpus there are only seven of them, all quoted in the box opposite. This is very few compared with the total number of oracles pronounced by the prophets. And if we also reflect that these seven 'predictions' are concentrated in the books of Isaiah and Jeremiah, we can say that this practice is completely unknown to the thirteen other prophets, and it is true to say that the task of the biblical prophet is truly not that of the soothsayer. Finally, we might note that for Jeremiah 25.11–12 and 29.10 the figure perhaps has a value which is more symbolic than chronological (seventy!).

The attraction of everything that is mysterious or enigmatic has always led through Christian history to a possible date for the end of the world, and people have never ceased to scrutinize the biblical prophecies in an attempt to find answers.

It is understandable that the approach of the third millennium should revive this genre of speculation. It is already important to be very careful in invoking such enigmatic texts as the one hundred and eleven sentences of St Malachias and the Centuries of Nostradamus. But the same prudence is also called for over the biblical texts. At the very least, time must be taken to consider all the prophetic texts and see the way in which prophets usually relate themselves to history. It is then easy to see how the biblical prophets, including John of the Apocalypse, have no propensity to divination or suggesting a calendar for the end.

Now that we have a better definition of what must be understood by 'prophecy' and have seen the importance of putting the prophets in their time and setting, we can return to the Apocalypse of John. The first task which awaits us here is to determine the probable date of the composition of the Apocalypse.

## A book of the 90s

The Apocalypse is often called 'the last book of the Bible', by reason of its 'physical' situation in the Christian Bible. Does that mean that it was the last to be written? Not necessarily, but almost. In fact the Gospel of John could be later. But the fact remains that we are referred to a period centred on the 90s.

As with the majority of biblical books, there is no conclusive internal argument for one date or the other. Traditionally we are dependent on the testimony of Irenaeus of Lyons, according to whom the composition of the Apocalypse will have been finished 'towards the end of the reign of Domitian'. Now Domitian reigned from 81 to 96, so the last decade of the first century will have seen the definitive redaction of the text of the Apocalypse. This is the traditional dating, and it is that suggested by the overwhelming majority of exegetes today.

That does not prevent our recognizing that this is a text with a history. Some scholars speak of two or even three apocalypses edited at different

## Five Dates to Remember for Understanding the Apocalypse

Working forward, we can say that the history of the Apocalypse is forged around five great events:

1. Beginning of the 30s: the death-and-resurrection of Jesus.

2. The 60s: the martyrdom of Peter and Paul and the persecution of Christians under Nero.

3. 70–73: the crushing of the Jewish revolt by the Romans, the capture of Jerusalem and the destruction of the Temple.

4. After the events of 70–73, increasing conflicts between Jews and Christians, ending up in an almost complete break around the 90s.

5. 81–96: the reign of Domitian, who continued to impose the practice of emperor worship, and for whom the Christians remained suspect and sometimes the object of persecution.

Chapter 1 has already stressed at length the place occupied by the death-and-resurrection of Christ in the architecture of the Apocalypse. It is possible to discover some recollection of Nero in certain features of the Beast (chs. 13; 17). Furthermore, the tragic events of 70–73 certainly played a very important part in John's reflections, and the disasters of which he speaks could very well be explained by what had happened in Jerusalem during these years which were so disturbing for Jews and for Christians who had come from Judaism. Finally, as subsequent pages try to illustrate, John pays special attention to the double conflict between Christians on the one hand and the Jews and imperial power on the other.

---

periods and brought together in the same volume at the end of the first century. What is certain is that in its definitive state the Apocalypse reflects more or less recent events or situations and proves to be an extremely valuable document for our knowledge of the church in the first century.

### A situation of extreme crisis

The apocalypses came into being at a time of crisis, or at least they perceive present or recent history as critical and tormenting. The Apocalypse of John is no exception. At the point at which he undertakes to give us his first vision, John leaves us in no doubt about the difficulties of the present moment: 'I John, your brother, who share with you in Jesus the tribulation and the kingdom and the patient endurance, was on the island called Patmos on account of the word of God and the testimony (literally the martyrdom) of Jesus' (1.9). Once we have become accustomed to some deliberate schematism, we can see how the letters to the seven churches in chapters two and three take account of certain tensions, divisions, sorry events within the communities: the conflict with the Nicolaitans for Ephesus (2.6), the 'tribulation' and the 'slander' of the 'synagogue of Satan' for Smyrna (2.9), the martyrdom of Antipas for Pergamum, the 'prostitution' with Jezebel and the 'eating of food sacrificed to idols' for Thyatira (2.19–20), etc.

More generally, John speaks of the 'great tribulation', on which he comments: 'They have washed their robes and made them white in the blood of the lamb' (7.24). This is an allusion to the passion of the Lamb (in the 30s) and the martyrdom of Christians (since the 60s). It is a crisis, an extreme crisis: three of the four horsemen (ch. 6) and all the trumpets (chs. 8–11) introduce us to a situation of distress, unhappiness and grave threat. The Apocalypse is a tormented book, and with good reason. The events which surrounded the persecution of Christians and the fall of Jerusalem produced sufficient horrors to inspire such discourse. We must not minimize John's testimony to this.

That is the general picture. In this situation of crisis, John keenly feels two particularly acute problems, which in a way come to structure the book. On the one hand, John and his community seek to define themselves in relation to their Jewish roots (mainly in chs. 2–11), and on the other hand, they loudly and courageously state their position in relation to the imperial power of Rome (mainly in chs. 12–20).

## Christians and their roots

It is not always easy to define oneself in relation to one's roots, and there are always ambiguities. We can see this right through the Gospels: Jesus has not come 'to abolish the law', but he is no longer its slave. While remaining faithful to his Jewish roots, he has opened a vast area of freedom and has broken through the constraints of a particular interpretation of the Jewish religion. The first Christian communities as described in the Acts of the Apostles still retain many connections with their Jewish roots: they celebrate Pentecost in Jerusalem, continue to pray faithfully and visit the Temple, cite ancient scripture, and so on.

On the other hand, we also see the birth of a Gentile church, with all the discussion which that was to entail, and the definitive move toward the pagans, begun by Paul and endorsed by the Council of Jerusalem (Acts 15). Meanwhile, increasingly frequent and serious clashes brought the Christians into conflict with the Jewish authorities in Jerusalem and with the different synagogues, and we can see a hardening on both sides, which developed to such an extent that at the beginning of the last decade of the first century the break between Jews and Christians was almost complete.

This serious problem of division and demarcation is the background to the whole of the first part of the Apocalypse (chs. 2–11).

Twice in the letters to the churches, John speaks of 'those who say that they are Jews and are not, but are a synagogue of Satan' (2.9; 3.9). So the whole problem is to know who the 'true' Jews are. And John's reply is that they are the Christians. The Christians lay claim to the same scripture, but they are aware of being called to form the new Israel.

Moreover, it is this transition from the old Israel to the new Israel which John shows as being in process of realization through chs. 4–11, which are steeped in the major symbols of the Old Testament.

Chapter 4: the twenty-four elders standing before the throne of the Living One symbolize Old Testament worship (twenty-four is perhaps related to the twenty-four categories of singers established by David: I Chron. 25).

Chapter 5 (see also ch. 10): the sealed book at least represents the Old Testament.

Chapter 7: the multitude of the saved grafts itself on to the considerable number of the Old Testament, largely represented by each of its tribes.

Chapter 11.1–13: the two witnesses have a power identical to that of Elijah and Moses, two names which alone are enough (cf. the accounts of the Transfiguration) to evoke the economy of the first covenant ('the Law and the Prophets').

Chapter 11.19: in a remarkably concentrated form the first part of the Apocalypse ends by evoking the three greatest manifestations of the presence of God among his people in the Old Testament – the Temple, the Ark and Sinai.

What is the aim of all this? On the one hand, we can see that John is introducing the dimension of newness. All these elements are shown in a new light and are surpassed by the event of Jesus Christ. But on the other hand, it is also possible to see an element of continuity: John still needs symbols from the Old Testament to define his faith in Jesus Christ, and for him the witnes-

# The Two Problems of the Hour

It is the beginning of the 90s. Less than twenty years earlier, the Jewish world had experienced the darkest hours of its history since the exile: Jerusalem had been put to fire and sword by the Romans, the Temple had been destroyed and the Roman domination over Palestine was now complete.

The Christians of Palestine and Asia Minor were deeply and grievously affected by these upheavals. For the most part they had a Jewish background, and had kept a profound attachment to the Temple; like Paul, moreover, they did not hesitate to visit the synagogues. However, after the events of 70 things changed. Isolated, official Judaism adopted a harder position and began to make difficulties for the Christians, which it increasingly regarded as a 'sect' (Acts 24.5, 14). These first confrontations with Judaism posed a dilemma to Christians: on the one hand they could not and would not deny their Jewish roots; on the other, how could they keep silent about the unprecedented novelty of the resurrection and the gospel of Christ? Chapters 4–11 of the Apocalypse seek to resolve this dilemma in their own way, showing the aspects of continuity and novelty of salvation attained by the Lamb.

A second major problem was that, like their Jewish brethren, the Christians had to take a stand over against Roman power, and above all the growing practice of emperor worship. Peter and Paul had already fallen victim to Nero's persecutions as early as the beginning of the 60s. One could say that the pages of the Apocalypse still bear the mark of the blood of the martyrs who, like them, bore witness to the Lamb and did not succumb to the seductions of the Beast: 'And they have conquered him by the blood of the Lamb and by the word of their testimony, for they loved not their lives even unto death' (12.11).

At the time John is writing (probably around the 90s), the memory of Nero was still very much alive, at least in the form of a legend. However, be this as it may, Domitian incarnated anew the excesses of a quest for power which led him to proclaim himself God and to persecute those who refused to recognize him as such and to surrender to the cult in his honour.

So before seeking in our modern world of the 1990s and the end of a millennium parallels which would allow us to say that, powerful and inspired visionary as he was, John described what was to happen for us 'soon', we must first note how far what he said applied to his own generation and could shed light on his contemporaries' views of their situation. Only after we have done this can we relate his message to our day, out of a concern to be faithful to the spirit and not to the letter.

ses and martyrs of the first covenant also form God's people of the new Jerusalem: 'It had a great, high wall, with twelve gates, and at the gates twelve angels, and on the gates the names of the twelve tribes of the sons of Israel were inscribed' (21.12).

## At grips with the Beast

The second part of the Apocalypse (chs. 12–20) touches on a problem of another order, but no less acute than the earlier one: that of relations with the imperial power of Rome.

After Augustus (27 BC – AD 14), imperial pretensions became increasingly excessive, to the point that the emperor became the object of a real cult. The emperors divinized themselves, or were divinized by their successors. Oddly enough, it was in the provinces – in Asia Minor – and not in the capital, Rome, that the cult had most success. And it is in cities like Ephesus, Smyrna, Pergamon, Philadelphia and so on that archaeology and numismatics have demonstrated the most evident traces of the practices of such a cult in Asia Minor.

The first century was particularly trying for Christians in this respect. There was a period of tolerance and moderation with Tiberius (14–37) and Claudius (41–54), but the sadly famous madness of Caligula (37–41) and Nero (54–68) was to push this cult to the limits of folly, provoking lively reaction from Christians. In the face of their refusal to yield, repression and persecution became increasingly violent. It was the recent past of imperial follies, leading to the persecution of Christians, which pushed the author of the Apocalypse to speak out in support of the position of his brothers in tribulation and to comfort them.

This was the recent past, which had become present again at the time when John was writing the Apocalypse. We have now reached the time of Domitian (81–96). While he was not as mad as Caligula and Nero, he nevertheless imposed the emperor cult, going so far as to call himself 'our Lord and our God' (*Dominus et Deus noster*). His letters had the heading 'Our Lord and our God ordains the following'. How could Christians who confessed 'our only Master and Lord, Jesus Christ' (Jude 4) accept any other claims? The emperor cult was incompatible with the Christian faith, and the Christians maintained a stand in the name of their faith. Even if Domitian did not practise a systematic persecution of Christians, they had very bad memories of him and spontaneously compared his reign with that of Nero. One thing is certain: the two-fold context of the imperial cult and the persecutions generally (under Domitian or before him) emerge very clearly from the book of the Apocalypse:

- 2.13: 'I know where you dwell, where Satan's throne is.' The church addressed here is that of the city of Pergamum, the main centre of emperor worship in Asia;

- 13.1–18: the Beast quite certainly has royal features; its image is set up and it seeks to seduce all the inhabitants of the earth into worshipping it;

- 14.8; 17.5 and ch. 18: as in contemporary Jewish apocalypses, the symbolic name of Babylon denotes the capital of the empire, Rome;

- Chapter 17: the allusion to the residence of the great harlot (the 'seven hills' . . . of Rome) and to the seven kings in succession refers us to a Roman imperial context;

- The numerous allusions to tribulation and the shedding of the blood of martyrs is quite understandable in the general context described above, which has existed since the time of Nero (1.9; 7.14; 12.11; 13.7; 20.4).

It would be difficult to find a more virulent criticism of the totalitarianism of the Roman emperors than that offered by the author of the Apocalypse in his imagery (see the box 'The Apocalypse, a War Book', page 23). In fact the Apocalypse is a real indictment of emperor worship. With all his monstrous imagery, the author presents the emperor in the most unfavourable light imaginable.

So the Apocalypse is born of a concrete historical situation, which called for a strong and clear intervention by a true prophet. John knew what he was saying by experience, not just from simple hearsay. He knew the torments of any Christian called on to take a stand against a Judaism closed to the innovations brought by Christ, sometimes even directly hostile, just as he had to suffer for his courageous resistance to the imperial power which required total submission and worship as though it were God. John was not afraid to take a stand in either case. His position is firm and courageous, but it always derives from a certain logic of the faith. It is always the mystery of the resurrection of Christ which explodes categories which others have tolerated or accepted.

The Apocalypse is a book of current affairs. But the current affairs are those of the 90s A D. Before we make it a book of current affairs for today, we must first see how it has succeeded in responding to the challenges of its times. We must not forget that this book was accepted by a commun-

ity and later included in the canon precisely because it responded to the questions, doubts, anxieties and needs of a community.

So reading the prophecy in the present, in the case of the Apocalypse, inevitably brings us back to the first century of our era. The 'events' evoked by the Apocalypse have already taken place as far as we are concerned. With the exception of chapters 21 and 22, which in a very clear way refer to the events of the end and a condition which the present creation does not yet know of, we have every reason to believe that the visions and revelations described in the Apocalypse relate to history contemporaneous with the author. In other words, for us these events are things of the past: a break with Judaism, the persecution of Christians, emperor worship, etc.

Certainly, it is always possible to establish parallels with our era: so many other eras have done so before us. But we must not forget that the author was writing primarily for his own time. And if there is any time to which the Apocalypse is relevant, surely it is then. Why seek to see in it an anticipatory description of modern times? Why seek to apply its names and dates? The names and dates are Domitian, the 90s (and doubtless the recollection of Nero, the 60s and the events of 70), but certainly not Hitler, Idi Amin Dada, the Ayatollah Khomeini, American imperialism or atheistic Communism. Nor, as far as these dates are concerned, is it the turn of the third millennium. John the prophet is not a futurologist nor a specialist on the year 2000 but a believer and a witness of the 90s! We need to learn to appreciate the great service that he has done his contemporaries in order to be inspired by the strength which animates him and to continue the battle that he waged so well. If we do that, it will be given us to live in hope and to prepare for the transformation of the present world, so that it takes on the colours of the 'new creation' promised by the prophet of Patmos.

## The Apocalypse, a War Book

The Apocalypse speaks more often of war than the rest of the New Testament put together: in fact it can claim fifteen of the twenty-five uses of the Greek root *polemos/polemeo* (= war/make war). What war is this? Essentially that which the Beast and the dragon wage against the believers and the saints (12.17; 13.7). In fact this earthly confrontation is the dimension of the battle between the Beast and the Lamb (17.14; 19.19) which is directly visible.

So John seeks to make believers more aware of what is really at stake in such a battle. It is not at all inappropriate to have a 'political' reading of the Apocalypse, in the sense that John denounces the idolatrous initiatives of the imperial power of Rome, while calling on believers to resist the assaults of the Beast: 'Who is like the Beast, and who can fight against it?' (13.4).

The Apocalypse is a real indictment against the imperial power. One could even call it a caricature, so unfavourable is the perspective which it adopts. All the images used by John show the monstrous character of this power. At the same time, John does not mince his words about those who have 'bestially' bowed down before the Beast (13.8, 13–14; 17.2); for him, these are 'cowardly', 'unfaithful', 'idolators', 'liars', etc. (21.8; 22.15).

A war book, the Apocalypse is also above all a hymn of victory: twenty-seven out of the twenty-eight instances of the verb 'conquer' in the New Testament occur in it. In effect it celebrates the great victory of the Lamb over the Beast and its royal partners (17.14). The Lamb appears here as the great victor (5.5; 6.2), while the Beast appears as the great loser (19.20; 20.7–15). Believers are also associated with this victory (17.14), and whoever 'hears what the Spirit says to the churches' could possibly be declared 'victor' with the Lamb (2.7, 11, 17, 26; 3.5, 12, 21).

# 3
# The Apocalypse in Figures and Colours: Learning the Symbols

## A forest of symbols

One of the greatest difficulties presented by reading and interpreting the Apocalypse is the way in which the author uses a wealth of symbolic language. He speaks through images, and calls on a spectacular range of audio-visual resources. To penetrate the world of the Apocalypse is to enter into a fantastic universe in which symbols are linked or clash, without ever giving the reader a break. It is almost like a twentieth-century video-clip.

With an ease which disconcerts the modern reader, John uses an impressive number of symbolic registers: colours and numbers; animal figures, sympathetic or monstrous; stars and the elements of the cosmos caught up in a profound upheaval; the plant and pastoral world centred upon the tree of life; the mysterious world of the heavenly court and the angels; or even symbols drawn directly from the religious and cultic language of the Old Testament.

At first sight it seems that there is too much, and that it may almost be impossible to see the wood for the trees. It all appears too complicated, too confused: we get the impression of entering a real labyrinth. And as we aren't sure of being able to get out again, it often happens that the mere sight of the symbols dissuades us from entering. That's a pity. For this is what makes up the wealth and originality of the Apocalypse.

Besides, artists, both Christian and non-Christian, have soon come to understand it and given us frescoes, paintings and mosaics, sometimes of a strange beauty, illuminations which excel in exploring the least details of the text: porches of cathedrals with sublime visions sculpted in stone; engravings and tapestries which project us into an unexpected world, and so on. Simply from an artistic point of view, the Apocalypse could easily lay claim to being its own museum. One could spend long hours, even whole days, there.

How can we fail to be fascinated by the original work which has inspired so many magnificent creations? Only a long and patient exposition of the original masterpiece can convince us. But once we are ready to expose ourselves to such a powerful work and to enter into dialogue with the texts, we shall soon become fascinated, and the difficulties which we imagined to begin with disappear.

## Symbols which are difficult to understand?

The regaining of interest in the Apocalypse has also coincided with a resurgence of fundamentalist readings. By fundamentalist readings I mean interpretations which 'reify' the content of the revelations made by John, and seek a literal and immediate reference for each of its details. For example, if the author speaks of a third of the sea, this must be understood in the strict sense, and one could measure precisely the impact of such a phenomenon. If he puts at 144,000 the number of those marked by the seal of the Lamb, the figure must be interpreted as given, without adding or subtracting a single unit. And so on.

Underlying this is a conception of the 'truth' of the Bible. For a text to be true, above all it cannot be said to have a 'symbolic' meaning. It is enough to take the text literally. This is amazing all the same, since John's text, the letter of the text, points us towards a symbolic sense. For example, in the account of his visions, John constantly appeals to comparisons: realities are described by 'as' or 'like'. He himself is well aware of using the language of images.

So to make a symbolic reading of the Apocalypse is not to do away with its truth by seeking to impose a mysterious meaning on it, a hidden meaning which it does not have. It is to serve the text, trusting the intelligence of the author and the coherence of his suggestions. Above all we must not say that the symbols are incomprehensible, since John takes trouble to show the significance of a large number of them.

Going from the known to the unknown, then, let's begin by looking at the symbols which are already decoded or deciphered by John:

- 1.20: 'As for the mystery of the seven stars which you saw in my right hand, and the seven golden lampstands, the seven stars are the angels of the seven churches and the seven lampstands are the seven churches.' So we must go beyond the words: certainly the author uses the words 'stars' and 'lampstands', but to denote other realities.

- 11.8: 'And their dead bodies will lie in the street of the great city which is allegorically called Sodom and Egypt, where their Lord was crucified.' This is Jerusalem, provided with unflattering nicknames: Sodom, the bloody and perverted city; Egypt, the land of oppression and slavery.

- 13.18: 'This calls for wisdom: let him who has understanding reckon the number of the Beast, for it is a human number, its number is six hundred and sixty-six.' God knows all the difficulties posed by the interpretation of this number. But we cannot say that the author has not warned us: 'this calls for wisdom', discernment.

- 17.5: 'And on her forehead was written a name of mystery: "Babylon the great, mother of harlots and of earth's abominations."' If Babylon simply meant Babylon there would be no mystery. Once more, the author invites us to look in another direction: he has Rome in mind!

- 17.9: 'This calls for a mind with wisdom: the seven heads are the seven hills on which the woman is seated.' We can count a thousand and one representations of the heads of the Beast, but basically it is again towards Rome and its famous 'seven hills' that we must look.

A second series of symbols is easy to interpret, since they are universal or quasi-universal. For example the 'great sword' given to the second horseman (6.4) undoubtedly represents violent murder and war. The use of the number four also relates him to a universal symbolism, to the 'four corners of the earth' (7.1; 9.14–15). So this is a way of speaking of phenomena of universal scope, affecting the whole of the inhabited earth.

A third series of symbols, the most important, is drawn from the Old Testament: the Son of Man, the tree of life, the hidden manna, the four living creatures, the Lamb, the book which is swallowed, the two witnesses, the Dragon and the Beast, etc. Here everything depends on the degree of our knowledge of the Old Testament: the symbols are charged with history. However, in themselves they are not enigmatic: for anyone who is familiar with the Old Testament John's text simply becomes more significant. And those who are not familiar with the Old Testament have a far from impossible task: they only have to school themselves in the Old Testament. One could speak of second-degree symbols, since they refer us to other biblical texts. But once this way has been traced, illumination is possible.

A fourth series of symbols is the fruit of John's own genius: he is the one who created them. But here again, there is a way of rediscovering the key, since John uses them in a sufficiently schematized way for us to be able to recognize them. I shall spend rather more time on this series, showing how John has modulated his message by an ingenious and coherent use of colours and figures.

Finally, we have to accept that the work achieved by the first four series of symbols still leaves some obscurities. Who could claim to interpret with certainty, in every detail, the seven heads and ten horns of the Beast (ch. 17)? But all in all, the proportion of obscure details remains minimal in relation to the symbolism of the Apocalypse as a whole. If the Apocalypse is a highly symbolic book, there are ways of understanding by far the majority of symbols used by John, provided that we are prepared to make the effort of comparing some of the texts.

A last comment on the symbols. Simply by virtue of their deep roots in the culture and religious universe of apocalyptic, they cannot all be transposed universally. I am thinking, for example, of the famous dragon of chs. 12–20: Chinese culture also sees this as a mystical monster, but there is nothing menacing about it there. On the contrary, it is an excessively sympathetic and popular figure. Like every biblical book, the Apocalypse must pass through the crucible of inculturation.

## A book with vividly contrasting colours

The Apocalypse is no dull and insipid projection of half-tones. Everything is radiant and striking. The colours could not be more vivid, and they are very 'typified'. This remark applies to the whole book, but nowhere is it better illustrated than in the passage about the four horses and their riders (ch. 6):

> [1] *Now I saw when the Lamb opened one of the seven seals, and I heard one of the four living creatures say, as with a voice of thunder, 'Come!'* [2] *And I saw, and behold, a white horse, and its rider had a bow; and a crown was given to him, and he went out conquering and to conquer.*
> [3] *When he opened the second seal, I heard the second living creature say, 'Come!'* [4] *And out came another horse, bright red; its rider was permitted to take peace from the earth, so that men should slay one another; and he was given a great sword.*
> [5] *When he opened the third seal, I heard the third living creature say, 'Come!'* [6] *And I saw, and behold, a black horse, and its rider had a balance in his hand; and I heard what seemed to be a voice in the midst of the four living creatures saying, 'A quart of wheat for a denarius; and three quarts of barley for a denarius; but do not harm oil and wine!'*
> [7] *When he opened the fourth seal, I heard the voice of the fourth living creature say, 'Come!'* [8] *And I saw, and behold, a pale horse, and its rider's name was Death, and Hades followed him; and they were given power over a fourth of the earth, to kill with sword and with famine and with pestilence and by wild beasts of the earth.*

Once more, we are well served by the context. Each of the colours reveals the activity of the horse and its rider. Let's begin with the last three. The second horse, bright red, is a synonym for murderous power and will put an end to peace on earth. Here the symbol used by John is related to a universal symbol: red is associated with blood and bloodshed. So we can talk here of a bloody power and think of persecutions and executions. The third horse is black. Although the description of its activity is vaguer, its basis is equally evident. A period of scarcity, famine and penury is announced. As for the fourth, pale horse, its rider's name leaves no doubt about his murderous intentions: he is called 'Death'.

The interpretation of the first horseman

remains the most difficult. Those who stress the links with the three others conclude that he too must announce some disaster. But it looks as if we must go in quite another direction, for the following reasons. First, when the white horse and its rider are mentioned again (19.11–13), there is no doubt as to the rider's identity: he is the Word of God. Secondly, his activity consists solely in 'conquering'. Now in the Apocalypse, this verb is mainly applied to Christ's victory in his resurrection. And finally, everywhere else the colour white is synonymous with good news and victory.

The table of colours in the box below gives a good indication of the way in which the author is not interested in half-tones. Two major colours occupy the forefront: on the one hand red and its derivatives (purple and scarlet), connected with the world of the Beast (bloody persecutions and debauchery), and on the other white, connected with the world of the Lamb and the resurrection. It is equally clear that of these two colours, white is the dominant one. Not an insipid, washed-out white, but a blazing white, gleaming and radiant. Through the torments of violence one can see the rays of a new world, illuminated by the power of the resurrection of Christ.

Is there any need to recall that it is John himself who asssociated colours and agents, and that the symbolism here is purely conventional? We have to remain within a logic established by John, without imposing on the text the modern con-

| The Symbolism of Colours | | |
|---|---|---|
| **Colour** | **Symbolism** | **Examples** |
| White | Divine world – resurrection – victory – dignity | The Son of man and his white head and hair (1.14) <br> The white stone of the conqueror (2.17) <br> The white garments of the faithful (3.4, 5, 18; 6.11; 7.9, 13; 14.14; 19.14) <br> Twenty-four elders clothed in white (4.4) <br> White horse (6.2; 19.11) <br> The white horses of the heavenly armies (19.14) <br> The white cloud of the Son of man (14.14) <br> The white throne (20.11) |
| Black | Disaster – distress | The black horse (6.5) <br> The black sun (6.12) |
| Red | Bloody power – violence | The bright red horse (6.4) <br> The bright red breastplate of the angels who sow death (9.17) <br> The red dragon (12.3) |
| Green | Death | The green horse (6.8) |
| Purple | Debauchery | The great harlot (17.4) <br> The cargoes of the merchants of Babylon (28.12) <br> The great city (Babylon: 18.16) |
| Scarlet | Debauchery | The same figures (17.3–4; 18.12, 16) |

notations of the colours that he has chosen. For example, the choice of white and black has nothing to do with racial questions, any more than green symbolizes hope.

## Rather special numbers

Even more than colours, numbers form a major part of the symbolic network established by John. If we read the book through, we shall soon become aware of the importance of numbers in general and John's affection for certain of them. In its use of numbers, the Apocalypse clearly comes at the head of the New Testament books, and in the Bible as a whole, only the Book of Numbers deprives it of first place.

So we cannot fail to be struck by the omnipresence of numbers in the Apocalpyse. The idea of primacy (Alpha – First) centres on the number one, there are two witnesses, three is evoked above all by its relevant fraction (a third), there are four horsemen, five months for the scourge of locusts, six occurs three times in 666, there are lots of sevens, ten horns, twelve gates and twelve ramparts, etc. All in all, John is very fond of sequences and quantities: everything is numbered and well ordered.

However, the Apocalypse must not be taken as a mathematically precise book. The numbers are there, but not just for their numerical value. Furthermore, in the Bible generally, numbers are regularly rounded up (seven, twelve, forty, seventy and a thousand): the aim is to give more of an overall view than a scrupulously detailed calculation. In other words, the numbers in the Bible give us an order of magnitude, but we must

---

## Talking of 'Numbers'!

Numbers have some importance elsewhere in the New Testament and also very often have symbolic associations. However, what is striking about the use of numbers in the Apocalypse is their frequency and their systematic character. This is how the Apocalypse relates, in this respect, to the other writings of the New Testament:

- The adjective 'first' (Greek *protos*) occurs 18 times as compared with a total of 92 for the New Testament: this total is the highest for an individual book;

- The adjective 'third' or 'a third' (*tritos*) is used 23 times out of a total of 48 for the New Testament (practically half);

- The number 'four' (*tessares*) appears 29 times out of a total of 41 for the New Testament;

- The number 'seven' (*hepta*), already known as *the* biblical number, is the author's favourite. He uses it 54 times out of 87 in the whole of the New Testament. The Apocalypse has more than sixty per cent of the uses of this number;

- The number 'twelve' (*dodeka*) is already well known from the Gospels (13 times in Matthew, 15 times in Mark and 12 times in Luke); here again, however, the Apocalypse claims the highest total: 23 times out of a total of 75 for the New Testament;

- The number 'twenty-four', itself a multiple of 'twelve', is exclusive to the Apocalypse in the New Testament;

- 'A thousand – thousands' (*chilioi-chilias*) is almost exclusively the language of the Apocalypse: 28 times out of 34.

not apply our mathematical rigour to them too much; otherwise we shall end up with nonsense. One of the best examples of the symbolic meaning of biblical numbers is given us by Jesus himself, who invites his followers to 'forgive seventy times seven' (Matt. 18.22): above all that does not mean that we have to forgive four hundred and ninety times! The idea is very clear: we must always forgive.

Let's look rather more closely at the general meaning of the numbers which recur most frequently in John's work.

First of all, the derivatives of three. Three itself is not used as an absolute figure. Rather, it is represented by the adjective 'third' in the enumeration of certain series: the third living creature (4.7), the third seal (6.5), the third angel (8.10), etc. and by the corresponding fraction, 'a third'. 8.7–12 will immediately give us an indication of this:

*⁷ The first angel blew his trumpet, and there followed hail and fire, mixed with blood, which fell upon the earth, and a third of the earth was burnt up, and a third of the trees were burnt up, and all green grass was burnt up. ⁸ The second angel blew his trumpet, and something like a great mountain, burning with fire, was thrown into the sea, ⁹ and a third of the sea became blood, a third of the living creatures in the sea died, and a third of the ships were destroyed.*

*¹⁰ The third angel blew his trumpet, and a great star fell from heaven, blazing like a torch, and it fell on a third of the rivers and on the fountains of water. ¹¹ The name of this star is Wormwood. A third of the waters became wormwood, and many men died of the water, because it was made bitter.*

*¹² The fourth angel blew his trumpet, and a third of the sun was struck, and a third of the moon, and a third of the stars, so that a third of their light was darkened; a third of the day was kept from shining, and likewise a third of the night.*

Here the trumpets announce disaster and destruction, for different spheres of creation: trees, sea, creatures, ships, sun and moon, etc. Such events are to be deplored: any destruction, even if partial, is regrettable. But it is important to put in perspective what is destroyed and what is preserved. Certainly disasters are announced and come about, but we should note that here only a third of creation is affected, not all of it. There are always survivors, and proportionately these are twice as many as those who are destroyed. By using a fraction, John indicates the real limits of the events which take place before his eyes. It will be the same with the death of human beings (9.15, 18): two out of three are spared. So the first third is synonymous with bad news, while the other two-thirds allow the best hopes.

Next comes the number four. This is represented above all by the figure of the four living creatures (4.6–8; 5.6, 8, 14; 6.1, 6; 7.11; 14.3; 15.7; 19.4), and then by the 'four angels standing at the four corners of the earth, holding back the four winds of the earth' (7.1; cf. also 7.2; 9.14, 15; 20.8), and finally by the 'four horns of the golden altar' (9.13). Apart from the last example, the rest are all connected in one way or another with the four points of the compass. So the intervention of the angels in question is seen as having repercussions for all the inhabitants of the earth. Four is the figure of the inhabited earth and thus, in a way, of humanity. It is doubtless also in this sense that the figure of the living creatures has to be interpreted: their identity remains mysterious, but they exercise a function over or on behalf of all humanity. The figure of the living creatures, too, should doubtless be interpreted in this sense: their identity remains mysterious, but they exercise a function over or on behalf of all humanity.

From all the evidence, the number seven is the keystone of John's numerical symbolism. It is omnipresent in his work from the first verses (1.4), with their mention of the 'seven churches of Asia' and the 'seven Spirits', to 21.9, with 'one of the seven angels with the seven bowls full of the seven last plagues'. All in all it occurs fifty-four times, and no less than a dozen different items are designated by this number. There can be no doubt that this kind of schematization is John's work. There are no series of six or eight: the sevens give him an ideal framework.

In fact the number seven is already well attested in the Bible as the number of perfection or plenitude: the seven days of the work of creation and God's rest (Gen. 1), the seven branches of the Mosaic lampstand (Ex. 25.31–37), the seven manifestations of the Spirit (Isa. 11), etc. In most cases the number 'seven' proves to be a number promising good things, indicating exellence, perfection, the ideal to attain. One particular Jewish tradition wants the number seven to be the number of perfection or fullness because it is the sum of three and four, the former being associated with the world of God and the latter being the number of the inhabited universe. Whatever the history of seven may be, it is certain that the biblical authors deliberately use it to create lists which they present as exhaustive or representative, whether positive (most of the time) or negative (to indicate the height of evil or disaster).

These different nuances recur throughout the Apocalypse. For example, when John refers to the seven churches, while he may have particular churches in view, he means above all to address the whole church of his time. When he speaks of the seven spirits he is always referring to the one Spirit of Jesus Christ but seeing it in the fullness and power of its various manifestations. In the case of negative lists, the idea of fullness remains, notably for the seven seals, the seven trumpets and the seven bowls. The misfortunes in question come to a climax. But it is useless to add them together and expect that they will strike one after another. If John chooses seven of them, it is to give a representative sample of the disasters which have happened recently or are going to happen soon.

Similarly, perhaps even to a greater degree than seven, the number twelve has an exceptional status in the biblical tradition. An enormous amount could no doubt be said about the history of twelve outside the Bible and in the ancient Near East, in relation to the months of the year and the signs of the Zodiac. It is no less certain that Israel borrowed from such a tradition. However, the strictly biblical history of the number twelve crystallized, from the Pentateuchal traditions on, around the figure of the twelve sons of Jacob, the ancestor of Egypt. A summary in Genesis 35.22 reminds us that 'the sons of Jacob were twelve', while another summary, at the end of Jacob's farewell speech, speaks of the same twelve sons, except that from now on it sees them under the sign of their collective destiny: 'All these are the tribes of Israel, twelve in number' (Gen. 4.28). These texts of Genesis are relatively late, but the tradition of the twelve tribes of Israel is very old (cf. Ex. 24.4; 39.14; Josh. 4.1–9).

So the number twelve has become a consecrated number: it is *the* number of the people of God. So it is not surprising to see how the biblical authors use it again spontaneously to describe objects which play a particularly important role in the collective destiny of Israel, above all – but not exclusively, in a liturgical context: the 'twelve stones' of Aaron's liturgical vestments (Ex. 39.14), the 'twelve silver plates, twelve silver basins, twelve golden dishes' for the dedication of the altar (Num. 7.84), the 'twelve cakes' offered on the sabbath 'as a covenant for ever' (Lev. 24.5–9), the twelve cubits square of the altar hearth (Ezek. 43.13–17), etc.

As an heir to this tradition, Jesus wanted to emphasize the continuity between the first covenant and the new covenant by calling twelve apostles to follow him: the 'twelve baskets full' of bread left over (Mark 6.43) indicate that the new people formed around Jesus will never lack the bread which he gives in superabundance.

If we now return to the Apocalypse, it is interesting to note that John keeps rigorously to the biblical symbolism of the number twelve, which he borrows from both Old and New Testaments. Chapter 7 leaves no doubt about his use of the Old Testament with the 12,000 of each of the twelve tribes of Israel. So we may under-

# The Symbolism of Numbers

| | |
|---|---|
| One – first | Exclusiveness, primacy, excellence: 'I am the First and the Last', 1.17; 2.8; 22.13 |
| Half – three and a half | Limited time, restricted period: silence of about half an hour, 8.1; a time and times and half a time (12.14); three days and a half (11.9, 11). |
| Four | Universality (the whole of the inhabited world): four winds . . . four corners of the earth |
| Six | Imperfection: 666 (13.18) |
| Seven | Fullness, totality, perfection: seven churches of Asia, seven spirits (1.4), seven golden lampstands (1.12), seven stars (1.16), seven burning lamps (4.5), seven seals (5.1), etc. |
| Twelve | Representatives of the tribes of the chosen people; continuity of the new people with the old: twelve stars crowning the woman's head (12.1), twelve tribes, twelve gates, twelve angels, twelve seated figures, twelve names, twelve apostles (21.12, 14, 20, 21) |
| A thousand | A large number, a multitude: thousands of thousands of angels (5.11); twelve thousand of each tribe<br>The thousand years (20.2–7): an extended period, a long time. |

stand the woman crowned with 'twelve stars' (12.1) to be the people of God, the messianic community which subsequently will be persecuted by the dragon but protected by God.

Finally, when the time comes to describe the new Jerusalem in chapter 21, John combines both Old and New Testaments in a splendid way: 'It (Jerusalem) had a great, high wall, with twelve gates, and at the gates twelve angels, and on the gates the names of the twelve tribes of the sons of Israel were inscribed: on the east three gates, on the north three gates, on the south three gates, and on the west three gates. And the wall of the city had twelve foundations, and on them the twelve names of the twelve apostles of the Lamb' (21.12–13). In other words, the new Jerusalem, which will also attract numerous people, will be rich in the long history of the people of God and in some way will mark the reconciliation of the two covenants.

A last number needs to have our attention: the 'thousand' used twenty-eight times by John. This tradition is manifestly a round number used to denote a multitude. The biblical tradition also shows considerable freedom here. If, for example, we take the first two chapters of the book of Numbers, we could say that as a census goes, the Bible has easy thousands! Similarly, when people vaunt David's prowess, they are not afraid of hyperbole, speaking of tens of thousands: 'Saul has slain his thousands, and David his ten thousands' (I Sam. 18.7). In each case it is certain that not all the units have been calculated rigorously. The important thing is to indicate an order of magnitude. To speak of thousands is to speak of a large number, a multitude.

Once more, John naturally fits into the biblical way of counting. 5.11 is an example: 'Then I looked and I heard around the throne and the living creature and the elders the voice of many angels, numbering myriads of myriads and thousands of thousands.' This is also the sense in which we are to interpret, a little later on, the one hundred and forty-four thousand of chapter 7 and the thousand years of chapter 20. To all intents and purposes the number 'thousand' plays the role of a superlative and could be translated 'many' or 'a very large number'.

## Three especially famous numbers

All in all, the general symbolism of numbers is easy to understand. But there are some more complex ones, the three most famous numbers in the Apocalypse: 144,000, the number of 'the sealed' (chapters 7 and 14); 666, the number of the Beast (chapter 13); and the 1000 which represents the number of years of the earthly reign of Christ and the faithful before the end of the world (ch. 20). These three numbers have never ceased to intrigue commentators, and have given rise to the most varied speculation.

## The 144,000 'sealed' (7.1–8; cf. 14.15)

Let's begin with the most impressive number, which is also the most important, since it relates to ultimate salvation and the partial or total number of the saved. To understand what is involved we should first recall the immediate context of the first mention of the 144,000.

We are still at the sixth seal: in other words, the disasters which it reveals are at the point of reaching their climax with the seventh seal, which points towards the horizon. But the beginning of chapter 7 is presented as a kind of interlude. After the 'four angels' have received power 'to harm earth and sea' (7.2), an order rings out: '"Do not harm the earth or the sea or the trees, till we have sealed the servants of our God upon their foreheads." And I heard the number of the sealed, a hundred and forty-four thousand sealed, out of every tribe of the sons of Israel' (7.3–4). Here we have a very important break in which singular, irresistible news bursts through despite all the rumours of disaster. But how far are we to see it as good news? Isn't 144,000 a very small number? And how do we know who is part of it?

The number has inspired a large number of religious groups, in our day as in the past, to preach the urgency of conversion. They take the number 144,000 literally and beg you to enter into the select and very limited group of those who want to escape the general catastrophe. As the number of places is limited, it is important to hasten to join the true church, the church of the 'pure' and the 'good'. Here appeal is made to the purest gospel tradition, since so many parables and sayings of Jesus talk of the lowly seed of the kingdom, the small number of the elect, the narrow gate and so on. The 144,000 of the Apocalypse simply needs to be taken literally: the 'small number' is now known to us with greater precision. If such an interpretation is correct, we can understand how a climate of fear can easily come into being: how could one be sure of being part of this 'small number'?

But in John's perspective is it really a small number? Don't people fail to read the whole of the context (7.9ff.), in which the 144,000 form only a fraction of the total number of the saved?

### Really good news

The first thing to say in connection with 7.1–8 is that it is essentially and uniquely good news. It is effectively a question of salvation. John borrows the term 'sealed' from the prophet Ezekiel (ch. 9): when the destruction of Jerusalem and the Temple is imminent, those who are 'sealed' will escape destruction because they have not been accomplices 'in all the abominations which are committed in it (Jerusalem)' (Ezek. 4). John also uses the same image in the same kind of context to signify the salvation of those who have not been accomplices of the Beast. So the 144,000 are certainly people who escape destruction and take part in the salvation achieved by the Lamb.

### 144,000 – a small number?

Now that the general sense of the vision has been established, we can return to the interpretation of the number itself. Has 144,000 to be understood in a realistic and exact sense, i.e. in the end of the day as a small number? The answer is no. We have already seen how the Bible generally is very sweeping in its use of figures and how it resorts to 'a thousand' to denote a multitude. To talk of a thousand who are 'sealed' is to refer to a large number. But the sum does not stop there.

For each of the twelve tribes of Israel, John speaks here of 'twelve thousand'. So the number 144,000 represents a very large number, since it is made up of the square of twelve (the number of the people of God) and a thousand (which stands for a large number). In other words, the 144,000 carries the idea of fullness: the people of God united around the Lamb will comprise, among others, an important representation of the people of the first covenant. 144,000 isn't a small number; on the contrary, in John's perspective it represents a considerable number of believers, men and women, descended from the first covenant.

## The total number of the saved?

And there is more than that. Too often, people stop at verse 8 and think that they are in a position to determine the total number of the saved. But the subsequent text leaves no doubt on this subject: to the important and representative number of the 144,000 from old Israel must be added an innumerable throng: 'After this I looked, and behold, a great multitude which no man could number, from every nation, from all tribes and peoples and tongues, standing before the throne and before the Lamb, clothed in white robes, with palm branches in their hands' (7.9).

So to preach conversion on the basis of a restrictive interpretation of chapter 7 of the Apocalypse is totally false to John's perspective. Once again, there is no question here of reducing the demand of the gospel and offering salvation on the cheap. Besides, one of the elders does not fail to recall in connection with this vast throng: 'These are they who have come out of the great tribulation; they have washed their robes and made them white in the blood of the Lamb' (7.14). Precisely that is the good news of the Apocalypse: the resurrection of Christ bears incommensurable fruit.

The God of the Apocalypse is not a mean or capricious God who has decided to count each unit of the saved and will stop at so precise a figure as twelve times twelve thousand: not one more and not one less. What a lamentable failure

this would be in comparison with the billions of human beings who have lived on this earth! On the contrary, the God of the Apocalypse is an infinitely generous God who keeps his promises: he desires the salvation of all people, and if we want to speak of those men and women who have been saved by the resurrection of Christ, John formally warns us that the total number of the saved is so high that we have to stop counting. That is John's real point of view. He does not preach conversion out of fear of finding oneself excluded from this small number, but conversion by faith in the power of the resurrection of Christ and joy of being part of an immense people without frontiers.

## The Beast and its number 666

Now we have to deal with the best-known number in the Apocalypse, and beyond doubt also the one that has been abused the most. We have seen everything – and its opposite. Enigmatic in the extreme, the number 666 reappears regularly to denote a being who incarnates the apogee of wickedness and is humanity's public enemy number one. It unfailingly figures in the repertoire of people who show some interest in Satan and the Antichrist. God knows how many lively discussions on this question there have been in the course of Christian history, and how this number has been used to denounce the enemy, to the point that the original has been changed (some manuscripts in fact have 616 instead of 666) in order to make it possible to attack other personalities. People still allow themselves purely arbitrary rules of interpretation to decry those whom they think the absolute incarnation of evil: depending on their allegiances, they apply the name of the Beast to systems, religions or individuals: the Roman empire, the barbarians, the papacy and the Catholic church, Protestantism, Judaism, Communism, American imperialism, Hitler and those who have recently emulated him.

Very recently there has been an upsurge of interest in 666. It is inscribed on the forehead of the boy Damien in the film *The Omen*; a number of preachers have spoken of a world plot which is said to turn on a computer code 666 (which people have wanted to see even in the computerization of food prices!); and it is by no means rare for acts of vandalism to be signed with the number 666 and accompanied by so-called 'satanic' slogans.

The first chapter allowed us to see the degree to which the Apocalypse is dominated by the figure of the risen Christ. If we have to recognize that the Beast and his number occupy a certain place in the book, we must not forget above all that they are far from deserving the whole attention of the reader. That having been said, John has certainly spoken of the 'number of the Beast', and we need to dwell on it.

First of all let's read the text and its immediate context (13.11–18):

> [11] *Then I saw another beast which rose out of the earth; it had two horns like a lamb and it spoke like a dragon.* [12] *It exercises all the authority of the first beast in its presence, and makes the earth and its inhabitant worship the first beast, whose mortal wound was healed.*
>
> [13] *It works great signs, even making fire come down from heaven to earth in the sight of men;*
>
> [14] *and by the signs which it is allowed to work in the presence of the beast, it deceives those who dwell on earth, bidding them make an image of the beast which was wounded by the sword and yet lived;* [15] *and it was allowed to give breath to the image of the beast so that the image of the beast should even speak, and to cause those who would not worship the image of the beast to be slain.* [16] *Also it causes all, both small and great, both rich and poor, both free and slave, to be marked on the right hand or the forehead,* [17] *so that no one can buy or sell unless he has the mark, that is, the name of the beast or the number of its name.* [18] *This calls for wisdom: let him who has understanding reckon the number of the beast, for it is a human number, its number is six hundred and sixty-six.*

Here more than ever, we need to proceed with a good deal of caution or 'wisdom', to use the words of the author. There is no question then of launching into an incisive argument and claiming to have solved an enigma which has given rise to so many divergent and opposed interpretations.

A first thing to do is to understand the kind of exercise that is suggested, 'reckoning the number of the Beast'. What does that mean? First we must understand the exercise and the rules of the game which, it must be confessed, were very much easier for John's contemporaries than they are for us.

In fact when John invites his readers to 'reckon the number of the Beast' he is suggesting a kind of charade. The only indication is 666 which expresses a total, a sum. What we have to do is to find a word or words, each of whose letters has a numeric value. By adding the numeric value of each of these letters we should arrive at 666, and at the same time, reading the sequence of the letters in question will give us the name of the figure or entity envisaged by John. To do that, of course, we have to know the language in which the author is writing and the values attributed to the letters of the alphabet that he uses. So in John's case we have to keep to the Greek alphabet, since his text is in Greek. Hebrew would not be inconceivable, since John thinks in Hebrew, but the basis for that is more fragile and hypothetical. It is better to keep to names taken from the Greek alphabet.

So what we have to know is that well before the Romans, the Greeks (later followed by the Jews) used each of the twenty-four letters of the alphabet to denote a number (see the box opposite containing the Greek alphabet with the numerical value of each of its letters). Each consonant, each vowel has its own numeric value. As a result it is easy to have alphabetical or numeric charades. One might say a name and ask people to find its number (i.e. the total of the letters which make it up). Or, as in the case of the number of the Beast, one could give the total number and give the reader the task of finding the corres-

# Numbers and Letters – Greek Style

| Letter | Name | Transcription | Numerical value |
|--------|------|---------------|-----------------|
| $A$ $\alpha$ | Alpha | a | 1 |
| $B$ $\beta$ | Beta | b | 2 |
| $\Gamma$ $\gamma$ | Gamma | g | 3 |
| $\Delta$ $\delta$ | Delta | d | 4 |
| $E$ $\varepsilon$ | Epsilon | e | 5 |
| $Z$ $\zeta$ | Zeta | z | 7 |
| $H$ $\eta$ | Eta | ee | 8 |
| $\Theta$ $\theta$ | Theta | th | 9 |
| $I$ $\iota$ | Iota | i | 10 |
| $K$ $\varkappa$ | Kappa | k | 20 |
| $\Lambda$ $\lambda$ | Lambda | l | 30 |
| $M$ $\mu$ | Mu | m | 40 |
| $N$ $\nu$ | Nu | n | 50 |
| $\Xi$ $\xi$ | Xi | x | 60 |
| $O$ $o$ | Omicron | o | 70 |
| $\Pi$ $\pi$ | Pi | p | 80 |
| $P$ $\rho$ | Rho | r | 100 |
| $\Sigma$ $\sigma$ | Sigma | s | 200 |
| $T$ $\tau$ | Tau | t | 300 |
| $\Upsilon$ $\upsilon$ | Upsilon | u | 400 |
| $\Phi$ $\phi$ | Phi | ph | 500 |
| $X$ $\chi$ | Khi | kh | 600 |
| $\Psi$ $\psi$ | Psi | ps | 700 |
| $\Omega$ $\omega$ | Omega | oa | 800 |

NB: All the letters have a numerical value, so one can find the total value, i.e. the number, of any word or expression in Greek. You will have noticed the absence of 6 from this table: the Greeks chose to represent it by a non-alphabetic sign.

ponding letters. We should note in passing that this kind of charade opens up the possibility of several solutions. One can play with different combinations of letters and numbers and arrive at the same total.

The first Christian generations had all they needed to solve the riddle. They were even inventive enough to change 666 into 616. So what is important is not so much to arrive at a solution (in any case no one has ever produced a solution which satisfied everyone) as to understand the procedure and mark out a certain range of possibilities. Here are some examples already proposed in the course of the first centuries.

In rejecting the 616 given by certain manuscripts, Irenaeus of Lyons suggested three names applicable to an emperor or the Roman empire in general: EUANTHAS, *ΕΥΑΝΘΑΣ*, LATEINOS *ΛΑΤΕΙΝΟΣ* and TEITAN *TEITAN*. Reference to the box containing the Greek alphabet allows us to see that the sum of the letters which compose each of these three words adds up to 666:

| E | υ | α | ν | θ | α | ς |
|---|---|---|---|---|---|---|
| E | u | a | v | th | a | s |
| 5 | 400 | 1 | 50 | 9 | 1 | 200 |

| Λ | α | τ | ε | ι | ν | ο | ς |
|---|---|---|---|---|---|---|---|
| L | a | t | e | i | n | o | s |
| 30 | 1 | 300 | 5 | 10 | 50 | 70 | 200 |

| T | ε | ι | τ | α | ν |
|---|---|---|---|---|---|
| T | e | i | t | a | n |
| 300 | 5 | 10 | 300 | 1 | 50 |

Although later and of less authority, some manuscripts sought to make things even clearer by replacing 666 with 616, as I have already mentioned. This would allow us, among other possibilities, to envisage Caligula (surnamed Gaios) or, more generally, Caesar proclaimed God (*Theos Kaisar*).

| Γ | α | ι | ο | ς | | Κ | α | ι | ς | α | ρ |
|---|---|---|---|---|---|---|---|---|---|---|---|
| G | a | i | o | s | | K | a | i | s | a | r |
| 3 | 1 | 10 | 70 | 200 | | 20 | 1 | 10 | 200 | 1 | 100 |

| Θ | ε | ο | ς | | | Κ | α | ι | ς | α | ρ |
|---|---|---|---|---|---|---|---|---|---|---|---|
| Th | e | o | s | | | K | a | i | s | a | r |
| 9 | 5 | 70 | 200 | | | 20 | 1 | 10 | 200 | 1 | 100 |

For people familiar with Greek the exercise could therefore produce a number of solutions, and that is what has happened. Without settling decisively on the personal identity of the Beast, in the light of the solutions found by the earliest commentators, we can recall the following guide-lines:

- First, priority must be given to solutions derived from the Greek alphabet, since John wrote in Greek. Ingenious solutions have been proposed in Hebrew and later in Latin, but they remain extremely fragile. All that we can be certain of is that John and his possible readers knew Greek;

- Secondly, the solution must necessarily fit the first century of our era: John envisages someone whom his public can recognize.

The solutions which point in the direction of later centuries down to the present day are sheer accommodations and often plunge us into pure and simple arbitrariness;

- The number of the Beast is to be interpreted in the widest context of chs. 12–18, and necessarily brings us into the sphere of Roman imperial power;

- The number of the Beast remains a 'human' number. Beyond doubt that can and may be understood in two senses. On the one hand it can be interpreted, understood, by the human spirit; and on the other it is confined to the human world in the sense that the Beast, despite all its efforts to make itself equal with God, remains a human, limited and provisional power.

## Can You Interpret the Number of Christ?

Like many other problems in the Apocalypse, our difficulty in interpreting the number of the Beast arises out of a lack of points of comparison. Now the number of the Beast was not the only one which interested the first Christians. So in a text slightly later than the Apocalypse of John another author plays on the letters of the name of Jesus and on the total of their numerical value: 'Then indeed the son of the great God will come, incarnate, likened to mortal men on earth, bearing four vowels, and the consonants in him are two. I will state explicitly the entire number for you. For eight units, an equal number of tens in addition to these, and eight hundreds will reveal the name ('Ιησοῦς = Iesous = 888) to men who are sated with faithlessness. But you consider in your heart Christ, the son of the most high, immortal God' (*Sybilline Oracles* I, 324–31).

### The thousand-year reign

Chapter 20 also introduces a number which has become popular in the Christian tradition, since it speaks of a reign of Christ and believers lasting for a period of a thousand years.

> *20¹ Then I saw an angel coming down from heaven, holding in his hand the key of the bottomless pit and a great chain. ² And he seized the dragon, that ancient serpent, who is the Devil and Satan, and bound him for a thousand years, ³ and threw him into the pit, and shut it and sealed it over him, that he should deceive the nations no more, till the thousand years were ended. After that he must be loosed for a little while. ⁴ Then I saw thrones, and seated on them were those to whom judgment was committed. Also I saw the souls of those who had been beheaded for their testimony to Jesus and for the word of God, and who had not worshipped the beast or its image and had not received its mark on their foreheads or their hands. They came to life, and reigned with Christ a thousand years. ⁵ The rest of the dead did not come to life until the thousand years were ended. This is the first resurrection. ⁶ Blessed and holy is he who shares in the first resurrection! Over such the second death has no power, but they shall be priests of God and of Christ, and they shall reign with him a thousand years.*

In connection with this text, let us recall the elements over which there is no doubt. First, this is good news: the victory of Christ, the defeat and chaining of the dragon who will be 'loosed' only 'for a little while'. Secondly, the witnesses to Jesus and the Word of God will participate in this victory.

The only questions which remain are 'when' and 'how'. Let's look at the 'how' first. Some preaching today tends to bring out the advantages or privileges which believers could have in the catastrophes surrounding the end of the world. It is enough to be among the believers, the converted, the good, not to be disturbed. Such an explanation does not fit with the logic of the present chapter or with that of the book as a whole. These are people who 'had been beheaded for their testimony to Jesus and for the word of God'. So they have paid the heavy price and have fully lived out the demands of the paschal mystery. And their 'reign' can only be of the same kind as that of Christ, i.e. founded on peace, justice and love. So there is nothing to indicate any privileges, or a 'rapture' which would remove Christians from the fate of humanity generally.

Furthermore, we must recall the extreme freedom with which John plays with numbers when it comes to the 'when'. A thousand indicates an important period, extended but not eternal. Can we know when it will begin and when it will end?

Apparently not. The difficulty with a literal reading is the uncertainty about where to start: does the count have to begin with the birth of Christ? With his death-and-resurrection in Jerusalem? Or with John? With the events that he describes? Or when his book has finally been written and received in the community? We can see how it is quite impossible to settle this question.

Besides, we certainly do well to remember that the church has never been millenarian. Millenarianisms have continually arisen in the church, and sometimes have enjoyed a degree of popularity. But they have always remained somewhat marginal and have never commanded the assent of the majority. It has always seemed wiser to adopt the position of St Augustine, who interprets this number as denoting the time of the church as a whole. The measurable duration of this time – which will soon be two thousand years – is of little import. The essential thing is to see that it announces the victory of Christ and the solidarity of believers with him in victory.

# 4
# Entering into the World of the Apocalypses

The Apocalypse of John is beyond question the most famous of all the apocalypses. To use a biblical turn of phrase, one could call it the Apocalypse of apocalypses. It is a model of the genre. Unfortunately, we too often forget that it is not the work of an individual, an eccentric genius, nor a new and isolated phenomenon from the literary point of view. On the contrary, a host of other writings of the same genre emerged before this work by the seer of Patmos, and others were to come in its wake, from both the Jewish and the Christian worlds, to imitate it or complete it, or even to show how distinctive it is.

If we are sometimes at sea over the Apocalypse of John, it is because we have nothing to compare it with. It is in fact very difficult to understand one apocalypse without having read others. Conversely, a greater familiarity with the apocalypses, whether canonical or non-canonical, Jewish or Christian, will allow us to appreciate each of them better, just as it allows us to establish parallels and trace a whole apocalyptic thread of procedures, images, symbols and themes. This comparison immediately sheds crucial light on what could be strange or inexplicable, and the impression of strangeness soon disappears. However, we have to be patient, since we need to read a good twenty works (granted, some are only a few pages long), the composition of which extends over almost four centuries, and the majority of which are com-

pletely unknown to the Christian public. People do not know what to make of works which are judged marginal and, who knows, perhaps even dangerous, because they have not been recognized among the inspired writings.

## A breath of fresh air for research

In our day, we can no longer allow ourselves to ignore the 'apocryphal' or non-canonical apocalyptic literature. Indeed, it has to be recognized that the reason why the study of the Apocalypse of John has progressed so far in a century is largely a better understanding of apocalyptic. For the moment, let us take apocalyptic to be the term for a literary genre which took off in the first two centuries before Jesus Christ, and came to an end in the second half of the second century after him. For a century now, the study of apocalyptic has been making considerable progress, thanks to the rediscovery and publication of a great corpus of extra-biblical works, Jewish or Christian, or both at once.

Even if there is no consensus on the definition of the word apocalyptic and the literary genre which it represents, the following points can be made. The publication of critical editions of individual works has made access to the texts easier. Certain studies already allow us to understand the historical background better and to risk comparisons. Furthermore, these texts are now

# What is Apocalyptic?

The word 'apocalyptic' has recurred a number of times in the preceding pages without it seeming necessary to give a precise definition of the term. According to popular usage, at least as an adjective it is understood to relate to the end of the world, or in a more specific sense to an apocalypse or the Apocalypse. That brings us back to the Apocalypse of John or other apocalypses, and in a way everything depends on discovering what 'relates' to these apocalypses.

One new development in the present chapter is the use of the same word as a noun. What do we understand by apocalyptic in this sense?

1. First of all it is a corpus of literature, a group of apocalypses from the Jewish or Christian world, spread out over four centuries around the beginning of the Christian era.

2. In an even broader sense, apocalyptic denotes a theological and spiritual movement ending up with or inspiring apocalypses.

3. One can also and above all speak of apocalyptic to denote the literary genre of the apocalypses, in which we can establish a certain number of constants.

4. Finally, apocalyptic can denote the science which studies the apocalypses, i.e. all research into the first three elements of the definition: the literary corpus, the theological and spiritual movement and finally the literary genre of the apocalypses.

What can we extract from the long discussion of specialists about apocalyptic?

---

accessible to a wider audience than specialists. They are available in the main modern languages. The twenty or so apocalypses which were relevant to the preparation of this chapter can be read in recent translations made by experts (for more details see the section For Further Reading).

One of the main gains of research has certainly been a rehabilitation of the apocalypses, comparable to the rehabilitation of the other apocryphal books. In other words, this literature is increasingly appreciated for its own sake, and its own distinctive logic is being recognized. We no longer have to justify the supposed symbolic or logical inconsistencies of the apocalypses. Apocalyptic has a language of its own of which we must be aware if we are to understand it, and not decry it from the start as deviating from the biblical traditions. The number of the apocalyptic writings and the duration of the period over which these texts were being composed puts us in the presence of a significant and by no means marginal phenomenon of late Judaism and primitive Christianity.

The study of the literary genre of apocalyptic has become quite indispensable. As we become aware of the vast corpus of texts grouped under the title of apocalypses, we shall quickly realize, at any rate, that the apocalyptic character of these writings is not the whole story. The apocalypses can also be parables, oracles, hymns or testaments (farewell speeches).

1. The Apocalypse of John is not an erratic block in the New Testament any more than it is a fantastic excrescence on the Jewish scene.

2. Is apocalyptic the daughter of prophecy or the heir of the wise men? It seems to have drawn more on the former, while incorporating elements of wisdom. Whatever it may be in origin, it strikes one as a particularly important medium at a time when prophecy seems to have fallen silent.

3. Research tends to make its definition of apocalyptic increasingly more precise, beginning

from formal indications rather than listing general characteristics.

4. The number of works listed in the box below is impressive: as I remarked, twenty have been taken into account here, and one could easily add around ten more which could claim the title apocalypse, at least for certain sections. Whether integrally or partially apocalyptic, these works shed significant, if not decisive, light on the milieu which saw the emergence of the Apocalypse of John.

5. Among all the apocalypses known and surveyed, quite special attention must be paid to three apocalypses which are contemporary: the Syriac Apocalypse of Baruch, the Apocalypse of John, and IV Esdras (Esdras is Greek for Ezra, and the work is also known as IV Ezra). They were all composed at the end of the first century (in the last decade) and essentially bear witness to the same events (those of 70–73) in Jerusalem, presenting us with three different perspectives on these events and on the role of the Roman empire in this immense tragedy.

Before we begin to compare the Apocalypse of John with other apocalypses, it is worth looking at the list of known apocalypses which can also be read in an English version. In itself it will already give us a good idea of the extent of the phenomenon and its distribution in terms of time and place of origin. The list has been drawn up from suggestions already made by specialists in apocalyptic. But it is meant above all to be practical: these are texts which can be checked out, and this chapter is based on study of them.

---

# To Help You Get Your Bearings

## I The Biblical Apocalypses

*1. The first sketches of apocalyptic*
Isaiah 24–27; Isaiah 65–66; Ezekiel (above all 1–3; 9; 26–27; 37–48); Joel; Zechariah

*2. The canonical apocalypses*
Daniel
'The Synoptic Apocalypse': Mark 13;
Matthew 24; Luke 21
The Apocalypse of John

## II The Other (Non-Canonical) Apocalypses

*1. Jewish apocalypses from the last two centuries BC*
Book of Jubilees (also called the Apocalypse of Moses or the Apocalypse of Adam)
Ethiopian Enoch (I Enoch) with the Apocalypse of Weeks and the Apocalypse of Animals
Psalms of Solomon
Testaments of the Twelve Patriarchs
From Qumran
Damascus Document
Community Rule
War Rule

*2. Jewish apocalypses of the first two centuries AD*
IV Esdras
Apocalypse of Abraham
Greek Apocalypse of Baruch (III Baruch)
Syriac Apocalypse of Baruch (II Baruch)
Assumption of Moses (or Testament of Moses)
Book of the Secrets of Enoch (II Enoch)
Sybilline Oracles (Books III–V)
Testament of Abraham
Life of Adam and Eve (also called the Apocalypse of Moses)

*3. Christian apocalypses of the first two centuries*
Apocalypse of Peter
Ascension of Isaiah
Sybilline Oracles (Books VI–VIII)

*4. Gnostic apocalypses from Nag Hammadi (Upper Egypt)*
Apocalypse of Adam
Apocalypse of James (I–II)
Apocalypse of Paul
Apocalypse of Peter

A look at this table suggests the three following comments:

1. The fluctuation in titles. We have to wait until the end of the first century of our era (probably until the Syriac Apocalypse of Baruch and that of John) to find the term 'apocalyptic' in the title of works considered to be apocalyptic. On the other hand, the phrase 'fluctuation of titles' is meant to indicate that several of the works mentioned are known under several titles: that is the case with the Book of Jubilees, the Assumption of Moses and the Life of Adam and Eve. Such a fluctuation of titles doubtless indicates the popularity of these works.

2. The duplication of works. We might imagine ourselves to be in the thick of modern cinema, where box office hits tend to be followed by a sequel. So apocalyptic literature has given us Enoch I and II, Baruch II and III (I obviously being the biblical book of the same name), the Apocalypse and the Testament of Abraham; and among the Christian apocalypses we find the Apocalypse of James I and II. In other words, the apocalyptic literature has its favourites and its great heroes, and at different periods of history there has been a concern to exploit the same basic material, taking care to adapt it to the taste and needs of the day.

3. The fusion of traditions. By far the majority of Jewish apocalypses have been preserved in Christian manuscripts. So we should not be surprised to see that they can include a large number of Christian interpolations or glosses. On the other hand, it is equally certain that the Christian apocalypses found no problem in importing procedures and traditions from the Jewish apocalypses. The frontiers are not always easy to mark out in this area. We should no longer be surprised, in the light of this phenomenon, to learn that it has often been asked whether the character of the Apocalypse of John is strictly Christian. Of all the writings listed, only those from Qumran come from a well-defined community. The others, by reason of a complex history of transmission, can reflect both Jewish and Christian traditions.

That having been said, let us try to discern the profile of the apocalypses more clearly (the section For Further Reading will help you to pursue this question further and put you in a better position to read or re-read the biblical and non-biblical apocalypses). Certain conclusions already suggested need to be restated here, but as far as possible an effort has been made to bring out features which have been left in the shade hitherto. However, the following remarks are no substitute for reading the texts: that is still the best way of entering into the world of the apocalypses.

## The historical context: times of crisis and excitement

The apocalypses came into being at a time of crisis, indeed what was thought to be extreme crisis. That is particularly the case with the earliest of the apocalypses that we know, the biblical book of Daniel, which brings us to the period of Antiochus Epiphanes (175–164) and the Maccabaean revolt (166–160). At the other chronological extreme, perhaps towards the middle of the second century of our era, we find another period of crisis, sparked off on the one hand by the persecution of Christians (see for example the letter of Pliny the Younger to Trajan written around 111–112), and on the other the crushing of Bar Kochba's Jewish revolt (132–135).

The some three centuries over which the apocalyptic literature extends represent, for Jews and later for Christians, a period which was both extremely tormented and singularly exciting. Let us recall some of the specific major events which gave rise to the apocalyptic texts.

In the second century before Jesus Christ, we can see a progressive Hellenization of Jerusalem, particularly under Antiochus Epiphanes, whose arrogance extended even to the desecration of the temple (the events of 167–164). Whereas some Jews wanted to fall in with these Hellenistic practices, resistance became organized with the Maccabees: 'A very great wrath came upon Israel' (I Macc. 1.64). This was a political resistance movement which also had a religious fervour, and gave rise to the movements of the Hasidim, Pharisees and Zealots.

In the first century before Jesus Christ, in 63 Pompey conquered Jerusalem and the Romans occupied Palestine. The royal and priestly power of Jerusalem was then under the supervision of Rome. The Essenes of Qumran, living in the region of the Dead Sea, made a complete break with the high priest Hyrcanus II of Jerusalem and with what one could call official Judaism. We can thus see a fragmentation of Judaism: Hasidim, Pharisees, Zealots, Essenes, Sadducees, etc. There were many factions, and also many messianic expectations.

For the first century of our era you need only refer to chapter 2, which has already given a full description of the historical situation which led to the production of the Apocalypse of John. And finally, the first half of the second century can be characterized, for Christians, by the continuation of persecutions and the rise of Gnostic currents (the Nag Hammadi apocalypses), and for Jews by the enthusiasm of the second Jewish revolt against Rome under Bar Kochba, and the bitter disappointment brought by his defeat at the hands of the Romans.

Those are the essentials of the historical situation. So it is easy to understand how the picture painted by the apocalyptists is somewhat sombre and tormented:

- For Daniel it is the 'abomination of desolation' (9.27; 11.31).

- Shortly after describing the death of Abraham, the Book of Jubilees announces an imminent (time of the Maccabees?) period of generalized corruption and devastation of the earth: 'For they all did evil and every mouth speaks of sin and all of their deeds (are) polluted and abominable. And all of their ways (are) contamination and pollu-

tion and corruption. Behold the land will be corrupted on account of all their deeds . . .' (Jubilees 23.17–18).

- The Essenes have particularly bad things to say against the transgressions of the covenant that they see coming from Jerusalem: 'The congregation of traitors, those who departed from the way. This was the time of which it is written, "Like a stubborn heifer was Israel stubborn", when the Scoffer arose who shed over Israel the waters of lies. He caused them to wander in a pathless wilderness, laying low the everlasting heights, abolishing the ways of righteousness and removing the boundary with which the forefathers had marked out their inheritance, that he might call down on them the curses of his covenant and deliver them up to the avenging sword of the covenant' (Damascus Rule 1.13–18).

- In a text contemporary with the Apocalypse of John, Baruch dwells for some time on the fate of Jerusalem: 'Blessed is he who was not born, or he who was born and died. But we, the living, woe to us, because we have seen those afflictions of Zion' (II Baruch 10.6–7). For him the pain is all the greater since he sees the prosperity of Babylon and the misery of Jerusalem: 'But now, behold the grief is infinite and the lamentation is unmeasurable, because, behold, you are happy and Zion has been destroyed' (II Baruch 11.2).

- John takes quite a different position and proclaims aloud the victory of Christ and the Christians and the fall of Rome-Babylon (ch. 18), but not without having described his generation as a time of 'tribulation', not to mention 'the great tribulation' (7.14), and not without having evoked at length the disasters which have struck Jerusalem (6–11) and the merciless battle waged by the dragon and the two beasts (chs. 12–13).

In short, the apocalyptists are sensitive to the internal crises of Judaism and Christianity and to the threats coming from outside: from Greece, when the movement started, but above all from Rome, from 63 BC on. Their cry of alarm is certainly not their last word, but expresses a situation of profound crisis. Where others could accommodate to the situation, the apocalyptists refuse to compromise and vigorously denounce the arrogance and the blasphemy of power, along with any form of submission to this power. Certainly their language might seem excessive, but there is nothing fictitious about it, and it essentially seeks to be a reading of the current situation.

## Writings of revelation

The etymology of the term 'apocalypse' has already brought us to the idea of revelation. Whether or not the word 'apocalypse' figures in the title of the apocalyptic works recalled here, their content of revelation proves to be most important.

Certainly the apocalyptists are not the only ones to do the work of revelation or unveiling. The biblical authors generally were already engaged in it, and the prophets had a very lively awareness of speaking in the name of someone, of transmitting the 'word of the Lord'. But the manner, and to a large degree the content, differs among the apocalyptists.

While the prophets had visions, they were primarily and above all men of the spoken word, and it was mainly their disciples who put their message in writing. With the apocalypses things are quite different. The visionaries receive the order to write first. They are scribes (Enoch, Baruch, Esdras), men of writing rather than of the word. And what they write is not necessarily accessible to everyone. Their revelations must to some degree remain 'secret'. These revelations rarely address an audience directly, other than the fictitious audience of the narration.

I Enoch, which contains poems and parables, is essentially a book of 'visions'. 'Enoch, the blessed and righteous man of the Lord, took up this parable while his eyes were open and he saw, and said, "This is a holy vision from the heavens which the angels showed me"' (I Enoch 1.2). III Baruch opens with the following phrase: 'Narration and Apocalypse of Baruch concerning the secret things which he saw by the command of God' (1.1). IV Esdras contains no less than seven visions, the interpretation of which is given by the angel Uriel or by the Most High himself.

John is in the line of Jewish apocalypses by virtue of the abundance of his visions (1.12; 4.1; 5.1; 6.1 etc.) and his concern to transmit them in writing (1.19). But the oral character remains present throughout, and the community is addressed. The best example of this is certainly the letters to the seven churches, in which each community is first congratulated, then warned, and finally called on to repent. In other words, these are no longer visions relating to times to come but a prophetic message addressed to communities contemporary with John. He also stands apart from other apocalyptists by the mission which he receives not to keep 'secret the prophetic words of this book' (22.10).

## The role of the visionary

One phenomenon which is easy to observe in a simple reading of a catalogue of apocalypses is that of pseudonimity. In other words, on the Jewish side the apocalypses are put under the patronage of ancestors from the past: Adam, Enoch, Abraham, Moses, the Son of Jacob, Elijah, Isaiah, Baruch, etc. These are names borrowed to lend more authority to the present message. In the case of the Christian apocalypses, there was a desire to find apostolic patronage: Peter, Thomas, James, Paul.

What about the Apocalypse of John? Is this a pseudonym? Perhaps. Is it John the Apostle? Tradition responds above all in the affirmative, but recent research, while recognizing some affinities between the Apocalypse and the Fourth Gospel, tends more towards the negative. At all events, in relationship to Jewish apocalypses John does not appear as a figure from the past.

He does not present himself under the cover of fiction, but under the sign of solidarity in the present tribulation: 'I, John, your brother, who share with you in Jesus the tribulation and the kingdom and the patient endurance . . .' (1.9).

This fact is quite generally recognized. But in reading other apocalypses we find another difference which is even more fundamental. It is what one might call the effacing of John. The apocalypses of Enoch and Baruch, for example, like the Testaments of Abraham or the Twelve Patriarchs, are full of anecdotal or autobiographical features. We find nothing, or very little, of that in John. John effaces himself completely behind the message. He is wholly at the service of the mystery that he describes. To tell the truth, it is more the Apocalypse of Jesus Christ (as we saw in chapter 1) than the Apocalypse of John!

One interesting thing is that his visions take place essentially on the same day, which is, in the event, 'the Lord's day' (1.10). Baruch, for one, has to spend days, if not weeks, fasting in order to be initiated further into the mysteries of the Most High: 'Therefore, go away and sanctify yourself for seven days and do not eat bread and do not drink water and do not speak to anybody. And after that come to this place, and I shall reveal myself to you, and I shall speak to you true things, and I shall command you with regard to the course of times, for they will come and will not tarry' (II Baruch 20.5–6). The same goes for Esdras: 'These are the signs which I am permitted to tell you, and if you pray again, and weep as you do now, and fast for seven days, you shall hear greater things than these' (IV Ezra 5.13). In both cases a progressive purification is necessary.

In John there is also a progression in revelation, but everything takes place in a single venue. Here again we can see the christological focus re-emerge. On the one hand it is the Christ, under the features of the Lamb, who opens the sealed book, and so John does not have to purify himself or make himself worthy to gain access to a superior knowledge. On the other hand, as everything happens within a very unified chrono-

logical framework, 'the Lord's day', it is still the central mystery of the Christian faith that holds all our attention: the numerous visions simply deploy different facets of the mystery of the resurrection of the Lord at work in the world.

One could equally speak of the effacement of John by virtue of the fact that he is nowhere called to play the role of intercessor. The Syriac Apocalypse of Baruch (3; 10; 11; 21; 48; 54), IV Esdras (8.20–24) and so many other apocalypses give us an interesting panoply of prayers addressed by the 'hero' of the book. In John, there are many prayers, but none from him. The liturgical acclamations are pronounced by the heavenly court and the multitude of the saved. In short, John effaces himself in two directions. Upwards, towards Christ, to leave him all the room. And downwards, towards the community, which expresses its prayers and its hope. There is nothing of the super-hero about John, the one who knows more than others and is better placed to intercede in favour of the people. John remains essentially a 'servant' (1.2), 'your brother, who shares with you in Jesus the tribulation' (1.9).

### The symbolism of numbers

The third chapter allowed us to note the considerable importance of numbers in the Apocalypse of John. As we have seen, this phenomenon introduces us to an exceptional case among the writings of the New Testament. Judgments become quite different when one changes the point of comparison and studies the use of numbers in apocalyptic literature. The apocalyptists are very fond of calculations and love to present the unfolding of history and the sequence of their visions in stereotyped numbers with a symbolic value. If we keep in our heads the numbers used by John, it is easy to see where he fits into a tradition which is already very rich in numerical symbolism.

II Baruch also uses the number four to denote the totality of a geographical space or the universality of empires, with the 'four angels who were standing at the four corners of the city' (6.4) and the vision of the four empires (39–40). On three occasions, Baruch devotes himself to fasting or a sanctification which extends over a period of *seven* days (the same idea of fullness and perfection as in John): 9.2; 20.5 (21.1); 43.3 (47.2). The number twelve (with one of its multiples, forty-eight) is also represented, with the 'forty-eight precious stones with which the priests were clothed' (6.7), the division of the time of distress into twelve parts (27), and finally the alternating vision of 'bright water' and 'black water' 'twelve times' (v. 6), and the 'twelve rivers' which came from the sea (v. 11). Finally, as in John, the exceptional fertility of the messianic kingdom is associated with the figure one thousand and its multiples: 'The earth will also yield fruits ten thousandfold. And on one vine will be a thousand branches, and one branch will produce a thousand clusters, and one cluster will produce a thousand grapes, and one grape will produce a cor of wine' (29.5).

From the Jewish part of the Sibylline Oracles we might above all recall the page which deals with the Roman emperors (we could remember here the section about Nero and his successors) and which, like John at the end of Apocalypse 13, plays on the numerical value (in Greek) of the initials of the different emperors (cf. the box above for the numerical value of the Greek letters: 'One who has fifty as an initial (= Nero) will be commander . . . even when he disappears he will be destructive. Then he will return declaring himself equal to God. But he will prove that he is not. Three princes after him will perish at each others' hands. Then will come a certain great destroyer of pious men, who shows a clear initial of seven times ten (= Vespasian, written *Ouespasianos* in Greek). His son, with a first initial of three hundred (= Titus), will get the better of him and take away his power. After him will be a commander, with an initial of four (Domitian), a cursed man, but then a revered man, of the number fifty (= Nerva). After him one who obtained a marked initial of three hundred (= Trajan) . . .' (5.28–42).

## The end is nigh!

The apocalypses are renowned for their reflections of an eschatological kind, to such a degree that in popular language the term 'apocalypse' has become almost synonymous with 'end of world'. But how far is this in fact the case in the apocalyptic texts? Indeed talk of the 'end of the world' or the 'end of time' plays a very major role in them. And no matter what portion of the history of Israel (contemporary or past) they comment on, the apocalyptists always envisage the end as coming soon.

The whole of the second section of I Enoch (chs. 37–71) contains 'parables' with marked eschatological resonance, in which the question is one of judgment and salvation, of punishment and deliverance, of assault and combat by the forces of evil, of the victory of the Elect and the gathering together of the exiles, etc.

The Book of Jubilees claims to cover the whole of human history, as the prologue indicates: 'This is the account of the division of days of the law and the testimony for annual observance according to their weeks and their jubilees throughout all the years of the world . . .' The author means in fact to give an account of all that is to happen 'from the time of the creation of the law and testimony . . . until the day of the new creation when the heaven and the earth shall be renewed . . .' (1.29). Although in his meditation on the history of salvation he only got to the time of the death of Abraham, he cannot help speaking of future history (granted, in relation to Abraham but also in relation to his readers), in accordance with a scenario for the end of the world: 'Behold, the land will be corrupted on account of all their deeds, and there will be no seed of the vine, and there will be no oil because their works are entirely faithless. And all of them will be destroyed together . . . Some of these will strive with others, youths with old men and old men with youths, the poor with the rich, the lowly with the great, and the beggar with the judge concerning the Law and the Covenant . . .' (23.18–19).

# The Biblical Roots of Apocalyptic

In this chapter our attention is on the non-canonical apocalypses, with which John shares an important number of similarities, though his work is also quite clearly distinct from them. At all events, it is important to recognize that already in the Old Testament there are passages with an undeniable apocalyptic colouring and an arsenal of images which are exploited by other apocalypses than the Apocalypse of John. In the case of the book of Daniel there are more than apocalyptic passages: in fact there we have one of the earliest Jewish apocalypses and the first canonical apocalypse.

Despite all that can be said about the differences between the apocalyptists and the prophets, it will always be the case that apocalyptic is a real 'daughter of prophecy', and that it is from the prophets that the apocalyptists drew to nurture and communicate their vision of the end.

Here I shall try to retrace briefly, in chronological order, the development of certain apocalyptic themes in the Bible, always taking care to see how they have been picked up in the Apocalypse of John.

The prophet Ezekiel, who was a witness to the exile (from 597 BC on), has the honour of having provided the first sketches of a systematic apocalyptic reflection, and it is to him that we owe the richest range of images and visions of an apocalyptic kind. In fact John makes abundant use of his work.

Ezekiel's vision of the glory of God (1–3) already uses to the full both animal symbolism (the four living creatures) and cosmic elements (fire, lightning, thunder, clouds and so on), and their deployment serves as a prelude to the manifestation of the glory (the throne, 1.26) of the son of man: these images find pride of place in John's presentation of the son of man (ch. 1), of the celestial court (chs. 4–5) and the theophany which concludes the first part of his book (the end of ch. 11). Ezekiel 9 conjures up the intervention of intermediaries charged with chastizing the city (six in number), while a seventh person is responsible for sealing on the forehead (9.4) those who refuse to be accomplices of the evil which is taking place there: we can immediately see the use that John made of the seal in his chapter 7. However, again in Ezekiel, it is above all from chapter 36 on that the prophet moves towards the events of the end: the restoration and even resurrection of the people (chs. 36–37), the final combat of God against the forces of evil (Gog and Magog, 38–39), the vision of the new Temple and the new City (40–48). Here too we find both the themes and the imagery which inspire John in his description of the fight of Christians against the Beast and the victory already attained in the resurrection of Christ, and the advent of the definitive city of God.

Another prophetic book, this time unrecognized, has left a profound stamp on John. This is the book of Zechariah, the first part of which (1–8) dates from the return from exile (around 520); the second (9–14) is clearly later. However, both inspired John. The first part, rich in visions, already knows the themes of horses and riders of different colours (1.8–13), the angelic interpreter (1.9, 11, 12, 14; 2.1, etc.), the golden lampstand and the two olive branches (4.2–3) and the seven eyes of the Lord (4.10) – all elements which we find again in the Apocalypse of John.

The second part (above all chs. 12–14) evokes the salvation to come and the definitive glory of Jerusalem which will come about after the victory of God over the idolaters. The prophet then speaks of scourges and terrible battles, but everything ends on a peaceful note: 'On that day there shall be inscribed on the bells of the horses, "Holy to the Lord" . . . And there shall no longer be a trader in the house of the Lord of hosts on that day' (Zech. 14.20–21).

Chapters 65–66 of Isaiah doubtless come from the same period as Zechariah 1–8, and they too played a decisive role in Israelite religious thought about the events of the end. Beyond question John sees things in the same way: he is closely dependent on Isaiah 65–66 and offers a particularly powerful Christian re-reading of it. It is enough here to recall the themes of the new creation, victory over death, unhindered prosperity and peace which will reign in Jerusalem, a new and universal worship, and so on, which are common to both Isaiah and John.

Around a century later (towards 400 BC), the little book of Joel (four chapters) presents a certain number of apocalyptic features. It knows the plague of locusts and disasters symbolized by horses (chs. 1–2). John combines the two images (Apocalypse 9.7). Joel envisages the Day of Yahweh as a formidable day which no one can face; John holds the same view (Apocalypse 6.17). John also borrows from Joel the image of the sickle and the harvest (compare Apocalypse 14.14–20 and Joel 4.13).

Isaiah 24–27 probably dates from the time of Alexander (333 BC) and has rightly been called the Apocalypse of Isaiah. The apocalyptic colouring of this passage results from the following elements: the perspective of the day of Yahweh ('that day . . .' 24.21; 25.9; 26.1; 27.1, 12), the announcement of a chastisement and devastation of universal dimensions (ch. 24), the anticipation of battle against the forces of evil (Leviathan, serpent and dragon, 27.1), the restoration of the chosen people (27.6–9) and the resurrection of the dead (26.19), victory over death and a festival for all the peoples (25.6–9). John has also made numerous borrowings from here.

Finally, beyond all contradiction, apocalyptic comes to a conclusion and culmination in the Old Testament in the book of Daniel (towards 150 BC). Although this book only has twelve chapters, scholars have felt able to detect in the Apocalypse of John more than fifty allusions or borrowings from Daniel (which is enormous compared with around eighty allusions to Isaiah, a book with five times as many chapters as Daniel).

Daniel remains a classic of apocalyptic. More than any other biblical book of the Old Testament, it presents itself as a written revelation which aims to unveil the mysteries of the future and the coming of the Son of Man. Its vision of the Son of Man appearing on the clouds of heaven (7.13, 14) develops one of the most original themes in apocalyptic. This magisterial scene is also included in a wider vision, that of the Ancient of Days sitting on his throne and surrounded by thousands of angels (7.9–10). To this two-fold vision of the heavenly world must be added Daniel's reading of contemporary history: this is essentially concerned with the attitude of believers who face the claims of the royal power. Believers must adopt a position to the cult that Nebuchadnezzar wants to impose: worship of the king's statue (3.4–7). Faced with such aberrant royal pretensions, the visionary cannot help comparing the power of the king with monstrous beasts which arise from the sea and put believers to the test (7.3–12, 17–26). The same images can be discovered in the Apocalypse of John (ch. 13).

John has been able to shape his message primarily from authentically biblical material, along with other apocalypses. And in the vast group of apocalypticists, he too engages in an original enterprise of re-reading the scriptures and bringing them up to date.

Beyond question Baruch, along with Edras, is the one who is most anxious about the coming of the end, as is witnessed by this dialogue which he has with God: 'And I answered and said, "But behold, O Lord, a man does not know the number of things which pass away nor those which come. For behold, I also know what has befallen me, but that which will happen with our enemies, I do not know, or when you will command your works." And he answered and said to me: "You also will be preserved until that time, namely until that sign which the Most High will bring about before the inhabitants of the earth at the end of days . . ." And I answered and said: "The tribulation which will be, will it last a long time; and that distress, will it embrace many years?" And he answered and said to me: "That time will be divided into twelve parts . . ."' (II Baruch 24.3–27.1).

Similarly, Esdras presses the Lord and the angel Uriel to know more on the subject of the end: 'How long are we to remain here? And when will come the harvest of our reward?' (4.35). 'If I have found favour in your sight, and if it is possible, and if I am worthy, show me this also: whether more time is to come than has passed, or whether the greater part has gone by' (4.44–45). 'Do you think that I shall live until those days? Or who will be alive in those days?' (4.51). The reply of the angel to this last question confirms Esdras in his convictions about the unfathomable character of God's designs: 'He answered me and said: "Concerning the signs about which you ask me, I can tell you in part but I was not sent to tell you concerning your life, for I do not know"' (4.52).

In John the eschatological note is certainly present with the mention of the Son of Man (in the inaugural vision), the wrath of God and the Lamb (6.17), the judgment (11.18), the harvest (14.14–20), the battle (16.14), the final victory (chs. 19–20) and the new Jerusalem (chs. 21–22). For him, too, it is 'what must happen soon' (1.1), 'for the time is near' (1.3). But one cannot say that John has any curiosity or attempts to know more, and he never affirms that the end has come. His

vision of eschatology also depends on his christology. In fact the 'end of time' is not in the future, so that there is a need to try to predict or foresee it; it has already come about in the decisive event of the death-and-resurrection of Jesus.

## Messianic writings?

The apocalypses came into being in a context of particularly intense messianic hope. So one might expect that the Messiah was one of the main figures of these writings. However, that is not the case. The figure of the Messiah is often more than discreet in them: apocalypses like II Enoch, Testament of Abraham, Testament of Moses and Sibylline Oracles III–V contain no reference to the Messiah, while the Apocalypse of Abraham reserves only a verse right at the end of the book (two verses from the end!) for him. Only the last two of the Psalms of Solomon celebrate the intervention of the Messiah. For these apocalypses, the final salvation will be the fruit of the direct intervention of God, or the figure of the archangel Michael plays a primary role. One can say that only a minority of apocalypses have explicitly stressed the role of the Messiah in connection with the events of the end.

I Enoch crystallizes its messianic hopes around the figure of a person whom it calls the Elect One or the Son of Man. It is to him that the final judgment belongs, with the Antecedent of Time, and it is from him that salvation for the congregation will come: 'On that day, my Elect One shall sit on the seat of glory and make a selection of their deeds' (45.3). 'The Lord of Spirits placed the Elect One on the throne of glory and he shall judge all the works of the holy ones in heaven above, weighing in the balance their deeds' (61.8); 'This Son of man . . . will become a staff for the righteous ones in order that they may lean on him and not fall. He is the light of the gentiles and he will become the hope of those who are sick in their hearts' (48.2, 4).

IV Esdras is certainly the most affirmative about the eschatological role of the Messiah: 'And as to the lion that you saw rousing up out of the forest . . . this is the Messiah whom the Most High has kept until the end of days, who will arise from the posterity of David, and will come and speak to them; he will denounce them for their ungodliness and for their wickedness, and will cast up before them their contemptuous dealings . . . But he will deliver in mercy the remnant of my people, those who have been saved throughout my borders, and he will make them joyful until the end comes, the day of judgment, of which I spoke to you at the beginning' (12.31–34).

On this point one can only reaffirm the remarkable singularity of the Apocalypse of John, the christological (= messianic) content of which is so rich. As we saw in Chapter 2, it is essentially a Revelation of Jesus Christ, i.e. Messiah. Of course it is not just that, since there is the Living One and the whole of the heavenly court, including Michael. But both the judgment and the salvation and the arrangement of the new Jerusalem are dominated by the figure of Jesus the Christ.

## Writings of consolation

Apocalyptic has the reputation of presenting a pessimistic, indeed a deterministic, vision of human history. That is one of the characteristics recognized by most, if not all, summary accounts of the subject. It is also one of the reasons which dissuade more than one reader from approaching such literature. We have already established as a first characteristic of this literature the tragic character of the views held by the apocalyptists. It is a fact that they pass a very severe judgment on their generation and that their writings have a wide range of terminology for scourges and calamities which will come to inflict humanity. But is this fatalism and determinism, and what is the ultimate aim of the apocalyptists? Are they indeed as far as is claimed from the tradition of the prophets, who certainly do not spare their contemporaries in any way but seek to influence them and to bring about conversion in them? Have the apocalyptists given up any attempt to influence

history? Do they despair of any conversion?

The dimension of consolation and hope certainly does not appear at first sight, but it is a thread running through the literature, and resists all the torment and anxieties which are on the surface.

At the beginning of the Book of Jubilees, God shows Moses the hardness of his people's heart and the innumerable infidelities which they will commit in the course of history. But everything ends up with a perspective of conversion, first revealed by God and then desired by Moses, who intercedes on behalf of his people. For God, it is the perspective of salvation which comes out on top: 'And afterward they will turn to me from among the nations with all their heart and with all their soul and with all their might. And I shall gather them from the midst of all the nations. And they will seek me so that I might be found by them. When they seek me with all their heart and with all their soul I shall reveal to them an abundance of peace in righteousness . . . And I shall build my sanctuary in their midst, and I shall dwell with them. And I shall be their God and they will be my people truly and rightly. And I shall not forsake them, and I shall not be alienated from them because I am the Lord their God' (1.15–18). Later, Moses receives the order to put in writing what will happen in the last days. The first part, quoted above, speaks of disasters and destruction, but the second opens on an exceptional horizon of salvation: 'And all of their days they will be complete and live in peace and rejoicing and there will be no Satan and no evil one who will destroy, because all of their days will be days of blessing and healing. And then the Lord will heal his servants, and they will rise up and see great peace. And they will drive out their enemies, and the righteous ones will see and give praise, and rejoice for ever and ever with joy . . .' (23.29–30).

I Enoch primarily and above all presents itself as a 'Word of blessing' for the 'elect and the righteous' (1.1), and the end of the book (from ch. 91 on) is a real crescendo of exhortations on the part of the patriarch: 'Let not your spirit be troubled by the times . . .' (92.2); 'Now, my children, I say to you: Love righteousness and walk therein . . .' (94.1); 'Be hopeful, you righteous ones' (96.1); 'But you, who have experienced pain, fear not, for there shall be a healing medicine for you, a bright light shall enlighten you, and a voice of rest you shall hear from heaven' (96.3); 'But you, souls of the righteous, fear not; and be hopeful you souls who died in righteousness' (102.4). Certainly this encouragement is interspersed with severe warnings, 'Woe to you . . .' But do we necessarily have to talk of dualism? Should we not see here rather a language of urgency, calling for a radical option? There is a choice to be made, now, but salvation is presented as possible: that is already good news in itself.

II Baruch ends with a letter from Baruch 'to the nine and a half tribes' deported to Babylon, who want a letter of comfort in their tribulation: 'But here also the word of consolation. For I mourned with regard to Zion and asked grace from the Most High and said, "Will these things exist for us until the end? And will these evils befall us always?" And the Mighty One did according to the multitude of his grace, and the Most High according to the magnitude of his mercy, and he revealed to me a word that I might be comforted, and showed me visions that I might not again be sorrowful . . . That is why, my brothers, I have written to you, that you may find consolation with regard to the multitude of tribulations' (81.1–4; 82.1). And if he has taken the decision to write, it is because he rejects fatalism and believes in the power of liberty: 'And these things which I have said earlier should be before your eyes always, since we are still in the spirit of the power of our liberty . . . Therefore before his judgment exacts his own and truth of that which is its due, let us prepare ourselves that we may possess and not be possessed, and that we may hope and not be put to shame, and that we may rest with our fathers and not be punished with those who hate us' (85.7, 9).

The Apocalypse of John also has as its ultimate aim the consolation of believers in the midst of their tribulations, an invitation to them to show courage and perseverance. It is essentially good news, punctuated by beatitudes and alleluias. The specific aim of the next chapter will be to show the 'evangelical' dimension of the book of the apocalyptist of Patmos.

t iudi quod aperuisse agnus      vit de sigillt· vij· q't tce cin spm tcin prtmis
unum de·vij·sigillt· hec est tcrtia ptc      ece u̅b̅r infundens· unus ans n̅ll mint

# 5

# The Apocalypse is Good News!

This fifth and last key, which we might call 'evangelical', derives from the first four, and to some degree confirms them and spells them out.

The christological key in fact brought us to the heart of the gospel by showing us John's profound understanding of the mystery of Christ, and it invites us to rejoice in the victory of the Risen One. So here we are at the very source of the unique good news which resounds throughout the New Testament. The historical or prophetic key brought out John's courage and the immense hope that he wanted to inculcate in a community which was undergoing sore trials. The symbolic key, applied to the colours and figures, also did not fail to pay homage to Christ's victory and to emphasize the fullness of life and power with which he is invested and which he shares with his church. In a stunning fashion it celebrates the immensity, not to say the universality and the unity, of the people of God. How can one not rejoice at this good news of a transformed Jerusalem, founded on the twelve apostles and in continuity with the twelve tribes of Israel, but going so far as to form 'a great multitude which no man could number, from every nation, from all tribes and peoples and tongues' (7.9)? Finally, the apocalyptic key also has its share of good news, steeping us in a particularly vigilant religious world which is preoccupied with the question of salvation and in which the intensity of hope results in repetitions

of words of consolation and exhortation to perseverance.

To speak of good news in connection with the Apocalypse of John is neither to make an *a priori* statement nor to arrive at a forced conclusion. It is a fact that is pressed home on us by the very force of the text, provided that we allow ourselves to be guided by this text rather than by the fantastic and alarmist speculations about our present generation and the uncertain fate of humankind on the threshold of the third millennium.

## A real New Testament writing

Before we begin our reading of the Apocalypse of John, we must tackle a question which many people have doubtless asked themselves. How did it come about that such a difficult writing got so far as to be included in the canon of the New Testament? Indeed, the book came up against some resistance during the first centuries, particularly from a large number of Eastern churches.

However, one fact remains: the Apocalypse of John was welcomed and preserved by Christians of the first two centuries as an important and inspiring writing, so much so that it could stand alongside such valuable works as the Gospels, the Acts of the Apostles, and the letters of Paul. So it was seen as an important and necessary work for nurturing faith and Christian hope.

Moreover, its singular position as the last book of the New Testament makes it the crown of this important section of the Bible, essentially devoted to the many facets and repercussions of the good news of Jesus Christ in the world.

### John, wholeheartedly for Christian happiness

A first reading of the Apocalypse usually makes people immediately aware of the roughnesses and difficulties of the text. But an exceptional light pierces these difficulties, in which happiness comes into its own and shines out in all its splendour. Far from being an overwhelming or depressing book, the Apocalypse of John bears witness to one who is wholly for happiness.

Faithful to his predilection for the number seven, John has found it very easy to scatter beatitudes through his book (seven in all) which are so many proclamations of happiness. First we should recall the terms in which they are formulated, and then draw some reflections from them.

The content of the box below prompts a number of observations:

1. In the New Testament, only Matthew and Luke offer a longer series of beatitudes (thirteen for the former and fifteen for the latter). With his seven beatitudes, John is on an equal footing with Paul. It has to be said that he comes out very well in this respect, and that if we leave aside the classical beatitudes of the evangelists Matthew and Luke, the Apocalypse proves to play a special role in defining Christian happiness.

2. The very fact that there are *seven* beatitudes suggests the idea of fullness. In other words, welcoming the content of the Apocalypse and putting it into practice should lead to perfect happiness. The happiness which derives from participation in the mystery of the Risen Christ is a happiness which fulfils all expectations.

---

## The Seven Beatitudes in the Apocalypse

1.3: Blessed is he who reads aloud the words of the prophecy, and blessed are those who hear, and who keep what is written therein, for the time is near.

14.13: And I heard a voice from heaven saying, 'Write this: Blessed are the dead who die in the Lord henceforth.' 'Blessed indeed,' says the Spirit, 'that they may rest from their labours, for their deeds follow them.'

16.15: 'Lo, I am coming like a thief. Blessed is he who is awake, keeping his garments that he may not go naked and be seen exposed!'

19.9: And the angel said to me, 'Write this: Blessed are those who are invited to the marriage supper of the Lamb.' And he said to me, 'These are true words of God.'

20.6: 'Blessed and holy is he who shares in the first resurrection! Over such the second death has no power, but they shall be priests of God and of Christ, and they shall reign with him a thousand years.'

22.7: 'And behold, I am coming soon. Blessed is he who keeps the words of the prophecy of this book.'

22.14: 'Blessed are those who wash their robes, that they may have the right to the tree of life and that they may enter the city by the gates.'

---

3. The first of the beatitudes (1.3) gives a framework for the interpretation of all the subsequent ones. The whole of the book thus stands under the sign of the beatitudes. What John writes and unveils is in no way aimed at provoking distress or fear at the magnitude of the crisis, but rather at sharing his conviction that the condition of being a disciple of Christ carries with it a vocation to happiness.

4. Twice, and like an echo, at the two extremities of the book (1.3 and 22.7), an account is given of the happiness of the readers or hearers of John's prophecy. While these are undoubtedly John's contemporaries, here the door is wide open to an unlimited public. Generation after generation of Christians will be called on to read this book and to find greater happiness through it.

5. Like the beatitudes in the Gospels, the proclamations of happiness in the Apocalypse have something paradoxical about them; they are not evident. Twice John is given the order to write (14.13; 19.9). This is a happiness which is revealed and proclaimed, which defies our human forecasts, but is nevertheless certain, since it is based on the authority of the promise and the Word of God (19.9).

6. And finally, we should note that the happiness presented in the Apocalypse necessarily takes on a paschal colouring. It cannot do without communion in the whole mystery of Christ: it is necessary to accept death in order to live. So there is no question of naive happiness, on the cheap, the result of good fortune. The promised happiness will be the fruit of a choice, and full and entire, courageous and joyful participation in the mystery of the death-and-resurrection of Christ.

## What about the disasters?

'This demystification is all very well,' people will say; 'It's all very well to speak of good news, but doesn't that ignore or play down certain passages which at first sight have nothing reassuring about them?' That's true enough: we have to admit that there is something formidable about the content of chapters 6, 8, 9 and 16. And to crown it all, there is nothing fictitious about the disasters conjured up here: they have been known throughout human history, and they can occur again. That having been said, we should keep several criteria of interpretation in mind when we approach the chapters in question:

The scourges in chs. 8 and 16 are sometimes described in terms very close to the story of the plagues of Egypt (Ex. 7–11). In fact, John evokes six of the ten plagues of Egypt. So it is very possible that John is not seeking to describe new realities, but rather to report what has happened in the light of a pattern he already knew: the plagues of Egypt. The intention couldn't be clearer: the tragic events of the 60s and 80s suggest the oppression once experienced in Egypt, but they are no less the heralds of a liberation of the people of God.

We should also take into account the question of literary genre. In this connection we must not forget that any self-respecting apocalypse has to have its list of catastrophes. That's part of the genre, and in this sphere hyperbole is easy. The apocalypses have a common arsenal of catastrophic events: famines, earthquakes, murderous wars, epidemics, etc. So John is not the only one to use such language, and he does not even offer the most terrible scenario.

Even if his language is steeped in imagery, we must not forget that he is translating a perception of events which have taken place, for him, since the 60s: persecutions, wars, exile, etc. As we saw in Chapter 2, the 'realistic' part of the events described by John focusses first and foremost on the period contemporary to him. We should not see in it a futuristic and fatalistic scenario according to which new scourges are going to break in on humankind in the year 2000. That is not one of John's preoccupations.

Once again, all these scourges are deplorable. Unfortunately, they have taken place and are summoned to happen again in the future. But as far as the Apocalypse of John is concerned, it is important to grasp that the scope of these scourges is always limited in space or time: destruction never goes above 'one third' and always extends only over a limited period: essentially 'three and a half months' (= 42 months = 1,260 days) or 'five months' (9.5). Furthermore, in his description of the scourges, John underlines their 'concessive' character; he brings this out very clearly in 9.1–5.

> *¹ And the fifth angel blew his trumpet, and I saw a star fallen from heaven to earth, and he was given the key of the shaft of the bottomless pit; ² he opened the shaft of the bottomless pit, and from the shaft rose smoke like the smoke of a great furnace, and the sun and the air were darkened with the smoke from the shaft. ³ Then from the smoke came locusts on the earth, and they were given power like the power of scorpions of the earth; ⁴ they were told not to harm the grass of the earth or any green growth or any tree, but only those of mankind who have not the seal of God upon their foreheads; ⁵ they were allowed to torture them for five months, but not to kill them.*

The passive which is used here is commonly called a 'theological' passive, in the sense that its logical subject is God. In other words, the destructive agents do not act on their own initiative, and receive very strict instructions and certain prohibitions. They are not the ones who dominate history.

Finally, there is never any question of a blind and absolute unleashing of the forces of evil. The author takes care to put them in perspective. The moment the trumpets sound (ch. 8), John first evokes the intercession of the saints (8.1–5): a prayer of compassion and a glimmer of hope, since someone, somewhere, is concerned about what is going to happen on earth. Once the trumpets have sounded, John introduces the figure of the two witnesses (ch. 10), and ends the first part of his book with the vision of the

temple, the ark and the theophany of Sinai (ch. 11). There are so many disasters so often only because of human malice and violence. But they cannot be the first or the last word in history. History is surrounded, framed, by the prayer of the saints and numerous signs of the presence of God with his people. They can hold their heads high and take courage: their God is there, seeing that the disasters do not bring them to the end of their strength.

### Towards a Christian vision of the 'end'

Now that we have recognized and applied the major principles for interpreting the Apocalypse, we have only to touch more specifically on the questions about a possible end of the world. These can certainly be found in the last two chapters of the book (21–22). But they are also raised through the book from the perspective of a dilemma: 'judgment or salvation?' Here again, though, John has not invented everything: he has his place in an extension of the reflection of the Gospels, more specifically what has been called the Synoptic Apocalypse (Mark 13; Matthew 24; Luke 21).

### The 'end' according to the Gospels

A preoccupation with the end is not alien to the Gospels. Mark 13, Matthew 24 and Luke 21 raise a question which was not just hypothetical. Overtaxed by the Roman occupation and driven to revolt, the Jews of Jerusalem and all Palestine were not sheltered from a Roman strike and could fear destructive intervention. The threat proved well-founded, and the events of 70 proved the most sombre forecasts right. The three chapters of the Gospels just mentioned echo this threat and the preoccupations to which it gave rise among the disciples. Now the response of Jesus is extremely illuminating in this respect.

First of all it has to be said that he firmly demystified the question. By refusing to give a precise date or to enlarge on the substance of such events (Mark 13.32), Jesus invited concentration on the present moment: 'Be on your guard, watch . . .' (Mark 13.33). Furthermore, all his parables of the kingdom relate to the present: it is *now* that the word must be accepted, *now* that one must love one's neighbour, *now* that one must discern the signs of the times and be ready for the coming of the king who has been on his travels, the bridegroom, or the master of the house who is late in coming.

The second demystification that Jesus achieves is that he does not say a word about those who will be responsible for such an end. While the disciples cannot think of anyone but the Roman authorities, Jesus does not accord them any role. The 'end' is not left in the hands of human madness, but rests in the hands of God, whose basic plan remains the salvation of humanity. Beyond the profound cosmic transformations, Jesus calls on people to turn resolutely towards the definitive fulfilment of salvation: 'And then they will see the Son of man coming in clouds with great power and glory. And then he will send out the angels, and gather his elect from the four winds, from the ends of the earth to the ends of heaven' (Mark 13.26–27).

The third demystification is that of fear. For Jesus it is a matter of course that the world as we now know it will be radically transformed. There will be signs in heaven and on earth. However, as Jesus says, 'the end is not yet' (Mark 13.7). In other words, these phenomena of a cosmic order are not the last word. They are not the whole story. The essential lies elsewhere; it is still to come: 'All this is but the beginning of the sufferings . . .' (Matt. 24.8). The sufferings are birth-pangs which announce an imminent deliverance: 'When these things begin to take place, look up and raise your heads, because your redemption is drawing near' (Luke 21.28). Far from engendering or nurturing fear, the perspective of the end is bright with manifestations of the kingdom of God, which is approaching its fulfilment.

## The 'end' according to the Apocalypse: judgment or the salvation of the world?

Reference to the end of the world in any religious discourse inevitably entails adopting a position on the judgment or the salvation of the world. What about this dilemma in the Apocalypse of John?

We can hardly deny the presence of the theme of judgment. There is even talk of the wrath of God (11.18), which 'destroys the destroyers of the earth' (11.18). It is also a matter of exclusion or excommunication: 'Outside are the dogs and sorcerers and fornicators and murderers and idolaters, and everyone who loves and practises falsehood' (22.15), and 'my recompense, to repay every one for what he has done' (22.12). Certain hymns even go so far as to call down in great cries judgment on the world which the just will see as a certain revenge on the part of God: 'O Sovereign Lord, holy and true, how long before you judge and avenge our blood on those who dwell on the earth?' (6.10). Such texts are quite amazing: they seem to bring us back to the implacable justice of the Old Testament, inseparable from a certain vengeance. However, as a counterpart the Apocalypse presents us with an unequivocal vision of salvation and universalistic accents which are among the finest pages in the Bible.

The initial address, by Jesus Christ, who 'loves us and has washed us from our sin by his blood', puts us in a perspective of salvation from the start. Each of the letters to the seven churches, after a vibrant call to conversion, envisages the possibility of a victory: 'To him who conquers, I shall give . . .' Then the liturgical acclamations open on the welcoming of a free salvation offered by God and the Lamb: 'They cried with a loud voice, "Salvation to our God who sits upon the throne, and to the Lamb"' (7.10); 'Hallelujah! Salvation and glory and power belong to our God . . .' (19.1).

The salvation in question in the Apocalypse is not reduced to a small number. Despite appearances, the number 144,000 (chs. 7; 14) does not

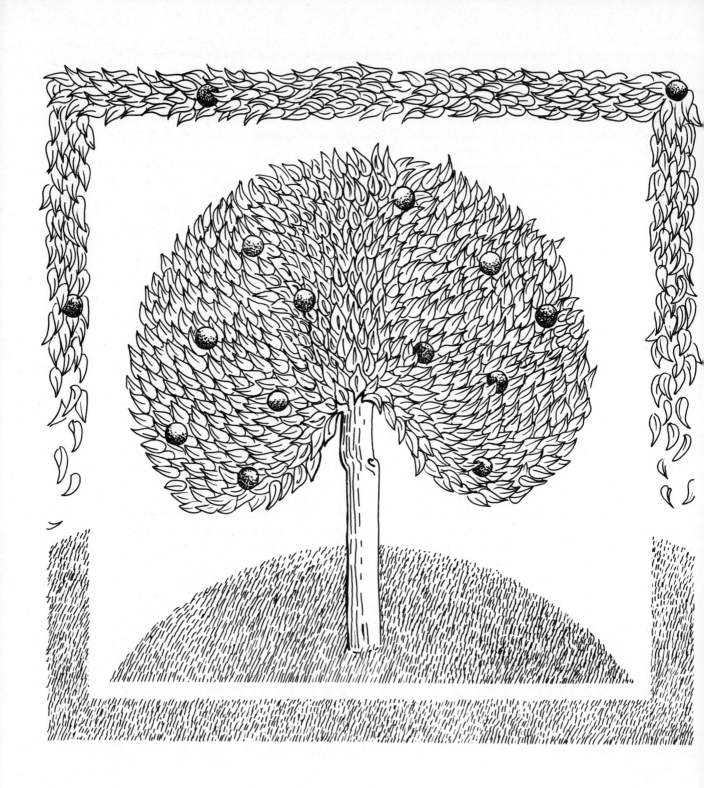

denote a limited number. On the contrary, it evokes an exemplary gathering of the multitudes which have come forth from Israel, the people of the first covenant (12 × 12 × 1000 = a very, very large number). To those must be added 'a great multitude which no man could number, from every nation, from all tribes and peoples and tongues' (7.9).

The universalistic perspective is further stressed: 'All nations shall come and worship you . . .' (15.4); 'By his light (of the Lamb) shall the nations walk, and the kings of the earth shall bring their glory into it' (21.24), and the foliage of the tree of life is 'for the healing of the nations. There shall no more be anything accursed' (22.2–3). So the Apocalypse transcends the narrow and self-interested perspective of an individual salvation, to project a light on to the collective destiny of humankind. And this destiny is the Lamb who comes to shape it, to illuminate it with his light and to heal it by his definitive victory over death: 'They shall hunger no more, neither thirst any more; the sun shall not strike them, nor any scorching heat. For the Lamb in the midst of the throne will be their shepherd, and he will guide them to springs of living water; and God will wipe away every tear from their eyes' (7.16–17).

## The new world of Apocalypse 21–22

Alarmist readings of the Apocalypse of John take delight in scrutinizing the most tormented chapters with their seals, trumpets and bowls, and the ones which describe the different murderous assaults of the Beast. Unfortunately they stop there, though the Apocalypse is a book on the move, and its meaning is not given until it ends. The tribulations and disasters are immense birth-pangs. The new world described at the end of the Apocalypse is what gives a meaning to all history.

One could not find a more beautiful fresco to represent the definitive future of the world. As everywhere else in the Apocalypse, the language here is highly symbolic. So there can be no question of reifying such a description (as if, for example, one were to expect twelve gates in paradise). But the Christian community has always found major co-ordinates here by which it can continue its way in hope, and work for the definitive future of this kingdom which it envisages. These major coordinates are provided by a wider biblical context than just the content of these two chapters.

1. Ample indication has been given of the parallels between these two chapters and chapters 2–3 (tree of life, First and Last, book of life, new Jerusalem, etc.). So we must use each to illuminate the other. On the one hand, the churches on their way through history and tribulation must keep on hoping as they turn towards the future which is promised them. On the other hand, for this very reason, the new creation is not just postponed to the last days. It is already present in the resurrection of Christ and experienced by his church. By connecting these two sections of the book closely together, John reconciles history and eschatology. Furthermore, we find this same encounter between history and eschatology in 7.14–17: the people who 'come from great tribulation' already enjoy the luminous and beneficial presence of the Lamb.

2. Chapters 21–22 are saturated with references to the prophets and, more specifically, to the chapters which conclude the prophetic books. These chapters are among the most open and the most universalistic in the Bible. There is talk there of a salvation with universal dimensions and manifested in the widest possible way.

John stands in the line of the great prophets. Like them, he denounced oppressive political power. Like them, he denounced the infidelities of the people and their compromises with the imperial power. But like them, his message had to be one of salvation. Where the people is sorely tried, God is made manifest and decides to intervene in a stunning way. The last word of God cannot be a word of destruction. On the contrary, it is a word of new creation ('Behold, I make all things new', 21.5); of gathering in and reconciliation ('they shall be his people – literally "his peoples" – and God himself will be with them', 21.3), of happiness and salvation ('He will wipe away every tear from their eyes, and death shall be no more, neither shall there be mourning nor crying nor pain any more, for the former things have passed away', 21.4), of presence and communion ('Behold, the dwelling of God is with men. He will dwell with them . . .', 21.3).

3. The last two chapters of the Apocalypse, and of the Bible as a book, admirably echo the first two chapters of Genesis. And this is no coincidence. The language of creation is explicitly used in them, as is a reference to the garden. Moreover, as in the case of the original garden, at the centre one can find a river which nourishes life, and a tree which is unique. This is no longer a tree to arouse human desire but a tree which will serve the healing of the nations, access to which is always open to human beings and with continual fertility: 'On either side of the river, the tree of life with its twelve kinds of fruit, yielding its fruit each month' (22.2). Eden is rediscovered for ever, for the utmost happiness of humankind.

In thus taking up the language of the beginning, John gives us a message of hope with an unprecedented power. According to him, the events of the end lie in the hands of the One who has created the world, and is said to have done all things well. Why fear? The end of the world is not the destruction of the world, but rather a new creation, in which the definitive victory of the resurrection of Christ will be fully deployed.

Almost two thousand years after the composition of the Apocalypse, we are still waiting for liberation from suffering and death. This is an expectation which is quite the opposite of passivity or negativism, since it is an aspiration for a new creation. It is a sometimes impatient expectation in the face of the injustice and suffering inflicted on so many human beings, but an active and joyful expectation, working for the re-establishment of justice, and calling with all its heart for the One who will make the universe new: 'Amen, come Lord Jesus!' (22.20).

| PROPHETS | APOCALYPSE |
|---|---|
| **Restoration of the people**<br>Zephaniah 3.18–21<br>Amos 9.11 | **Restoration of the people**<br>New Jerusalem (21.2)<br>Twelve gates/tribes (21.12) |
| **Universalism**<br>Isaiah 66.18–20, 23<br>Zephaniah 3.9–10 | **Universalism**<br>HIS PEOPLES (21.3)<br>The nations (21.24) |
| **Peace and happiness**<br>Amos 9.13–15<br>Isaiah 65.21–25 | **Peace and happiness**<br>Abolition of death (21.4)<br>Tree of life (22.2) |
| **New creation**<br>Isaiah 65.17<br>Ezekiel (47.12) | **New creation**<br>New heaven (21.1)<br>God recreates everything (21.5) |
| **New city**<br>Isaiah 65.18–19<br>Micah 4.1–5 | **New city**<br>God's dwelling (21.2–3)<br>Holy city (21.9–27) |
| **Liturgy without frontiers**<br>Isaiah 66.21–23<br>Micah 4.1–5 | **Liturgy without frontiers**<br>The coming of the nations (21.24)<br>The glory of God (21.6, 22–23) |
| **Presence of God**<br>Zephaniah 3.14–17 | **Presence of God**<br>God-with-them (21.3)<br>No more temple . . . (21.22–23) |

# PART TWO

# STUDYING TEXTS

Part One has shown us the major principles of interpretation on which a wide range of Christian exegetes who have studied the Apocalypse are at present generally agreed. And each of these principles (the keys to interpretation) has led us each time to consider the whole of the book.

In Part Two, we shall now go on to examine the text from another angle: that of chapters and literary units. You should not, however, expect to find a classical 'commentary' here, verse by verse and word by word. That work has already been done, and you will find a list of good commentaries on the Apocalypse in the bibliography at the end of this book. Nor can there be any question of considering all twenty-two chapters of the Apocalypse, which would take us far beyond the limits of a book in this series.

All in all, we shall be looking at nine chapters. The study of these nine chapters has proved a fascinating enterprise, and whets one's appetite to go on to look at the other thirteen. At all events, it brings out the extraordinary unity of John's work and the exceptional network of parallels which bear witness to the power of his genius. Remember that the aim of the commentary which follows is not to shed philological light on words or verses but to grasp the distinctive dynamism of certain literary units, and the message which emerges from these units.

Since so many chapters have had to be left aside, the question of the criteria of selection is a legitimate one. The choice of chapters 3 to 7, 12 and 21–22 should not pose any problem: these are well-known texts, and among the most quoted from the Apocalypse. However, I have attempted to present them in a new light. The chapters which I have omitted often have close links with the chapters presented here, so that the same principles of interpretation could easily be applied to them. The most striking example of this is the series of seven trumpets (8–9) and bowls (16), which can easily be understood by referring to the study of the first series of seven which is included here (6–7).

Furthermore, on page 116, you will find a box entitled 'How to Study the Rest of the Apocalypse' which you can use to relate the pointers given here to the other chapters of the Apocalypse which have not been covered.

# 6

# Hear what the Spirit says to the Churches . . .

## (Apocalypse 2–3)

The reticence usually felt by the very mention of the word 'Apocalypse' soon disappears when one begins these two chapters which are traditionally called the 'letters to the seven churches' (2–3). The two chapters are so lucid and easy to apply that the mischievous will say that there is nothing apocalyptic about them and that they could have existed independently, before being turned into a work of quite a different kind. It is true that these two chapters are deeply compelling and that they have everything to say to today's church, but now that we have made a general survey of John's book, how could we think of making their prophetic distinctiveness a special feature which distinguishes them from the rest of the Apocalypse?

### An autonomous and independent collection . . .?

Struck by the numerous literary and symbolic differences, at the beginning of this century commentators saw Apocalypse 2–3 as an autonomous literary block, which could have pre-existed the present text of the Apocalypse. At that time there was a tendency to see them as real letters, actually sent to the various communities concerned and received in the order in which they appear.

Even if today the common standpoint of researchers is quite the opposite, we have to recognize a certain number of differences. From a literary point of view these two chapters present an unusual concentration of stereotyped formulas: 'To the angel of the church of . . . write': 'The words of the . . .', 'I know', 'But I have this against you . . .', 'Repent . . .', 'To him who conquers . . .' and finally, 'He who has an ear, let him hear what the Spirit says to the churches.' John uses many stereotyped formulae right through his book here, but what is surprising is the marked concentration in passages which average only six or seven verses. There is also a certain number of grammatical and stylistic peculiarities, but since the present study is not addressed to specialists in Greek, it is enough simply to state the fact without demonstrating it.

On the other hand, there are no less remarkable differences in content and symbolism. First of all what is not there: chapters 2 and 3 know nothing of spectacular theophanies, fantastic animals and the cosmic battle which we shall find later on. Nor do we find any doxology or any hymns. However, on the positive side, it is in this section of the book that Christ speaks most often and at the greatest length. He does so in prophetic fashion, inviting the churches either to conversion or to faithfulness and perseverance.

### . . . or an essential key to the book?

Over recent decades, scholars have rightly

# Apocalypse 2–3

| | EPHESUS (2.1–7) | SMYRNA (2.8–11) | PERGAMUM (2.12–17) | THYATIRA (2.18–29) | SARDES (3.1–6) | PHILA-DELPHIA (3.7–13) | LAODICEA 3.14–22) |
|---|---|---|---|---|---|---|---|
| | 1 | 2 | 3 | 4 | 5 | 6 | 7 |
| ADDRESS | To the angel of the church in Ephesus write | To the angel of the church in Smyrna write | To the angel of the church in Pergamum write | To the angel of the church in Thyatira write | To the angel of the church in Sardes write | To the angel of the church in Phila-delphia write | To the angel of the church in Laodicea write |
| CHRIST | he who holds the seven stars in his right hand, who walks among the seven golden lampstands | the first and the last, who died and came to life | who has the sharp two-edged sword | the Son of God, who has eyes like a flame of fire, and whose feet are like burnished bronze | he who has the seven spirits of God and the seven stars | the holy one, the true one, who has the key of David | the Amen, the faithful and true witness, the beginning of God's creation |
| JUDGMENT | + works + endurance + hate of the Nicolaitans — abandoned the love you had at first | + tribulation + poverty = riches | + holding fast in faith + martyrdom of Antipas — teaching of Balaam and the Nicolaitans | + love, faith, devotion, endurance [− tolerance of Jezebel] | + faithfulness of some — life = death | + faithfulness to the word and the name of Christ | — lukewarm — riches = poverty |
| CONVER-SION | Repent (twice) | Do not fear, be faithful | Repent | [get Jezebel to repent] | Repent | Hold fast | Repent |
| HEAR | He who has an ear, let him hear what the Spirit says to the churches | He who has an ear, let him hear what the Spirit says to the churches | He who has an ear, let him hear what the Spirit says to the churches | He who has an ear, let him hear what the Spirit says to the churches | He who has an ear, let him hear what the Spirit says to the churches | He who has an ear, let him hear what the Spirit says to the churches | He who has an ear, let him hear what the Spirit says to the churches |
| PROMISE | Eat of the tree of life, which is in the paradise of God | Crown of life, deliver-ance from the second death | Hidden manna, white stone, new name | Power over the nations, morning star | White garments Name in the book of life | Pillar in the temple Name of God New Jerusalem New name | Eat with Christ Sit with Christ on his throne |

insisted that chapters 2 and 3 are part of the book as a whole. Constructed after the rest of the book, these two chapters are steeped in what has gone before and what comes after, and we find the main themes of the book concentrated in them.

On the one hand, the two chapters flow directly from the first chapter, and above all from the inaugural vision of the Son of Man. The address in 1.4 and the account of the vision (1.11, 20) already refer to the 'seven churches' (individually named in 1.11). Furthermore, and this is doubtless the most important feature, all the proclamations of chs. 2–3, except for that to the church of Philadelphia, take up one or more christological titles from the initial vision. And finally, two other themes from the first chapter are echoed in chs. 2–3: the '(golden) lamp-stands' (1.12–13, 20, which is taken up in 2.1, 5) and the 'sword' (1.16, which is taken up in 2.16).

On the other hand, as has already been stressed in Part One, chapters 2–3 anticipate more than one feature of the new Jerusalem (21–22), in the promise which is made to the one who conquers, access to the tree of life (2.7; 22.2, 14), deliverance from the second death (2.11 and 21.8) and the appearance of the new Jerusalem (3.12; 21.2). To this we must add the giving of a new name (2.17; 9.12) and finally the reference to the churches (22.16).

So chapters 2 and 3 are very much part of the Apocalypse. With their distinctive features they fit admirably into the great fresco of the book, from which they cannot be detached, and for which they provide an essential key. It is to the 'seven churches' that John is ordered to write, not only the seven 'letters' but all that he sees (1.11).

## Proper letters . . .?

It is traditional to speak of 'letters' to the seven churches, and for that reason this is the easiest way of referring to chapters 2 and 3. But when we look closer, we have to accept that the term does not mean much from a literary point of view. In fact, if we compare chapters 2 and 3 with the epistolary genre of primitive Christianity, attested in the letters of Peter, Paul, James and John, or even Clement of Rome and Ignatius of Antioch, we do not find in them the elements which form a letter: initial salutation and wishes, the occasion for the letter, final salutation. What seems to lie behind the traditional nomenclature is the order to write, which appears in each of the 'letters'. But it has to be said that one can write other things than letters, and this is the case throughout the Apocalypse, since John is ordered to write a book to be sent to the seven churches (1.11), and its whole content, and therefore that of the whole of the Book of the Apocalypse, is addressed to the seven churches (1.4, 11; 22.16). It also has to be said that there are more signs of an epistolary character elsewhere in the book, for example in the inaugural address and salutation: 'John to the seven churches that are in Asia: Grace to you and peace from him who is and was and who is to come, and from the seven spirits who are before his throne, and from Jesus Christ the faithful witness, the firstborn of the dead, and the ruler of kings on earth. To him who loves us and has freed us from our sins by his blood . . .' (1.4–5); in the way in which John introduces himself: 'I, John, your brother, who share with you in Jesus the tribulation and the kingdom and the patient endurance, was on the island called Patmos on account of the word of God and the testimony of Jesus' (1.9); and in the final salutation: 'The grace of the Lord Jesus be with you all! Amen' (22.21).

## . . . or prophetic oracles

We have to go further than a designation like letters, which is too generic and in fact inappropriate, to account for the literary genre of each of the proclamations addressed to the seven churches. They clearly have a prophetic tenor and twist. Moreover, in form and basis they have connections with prophetic oracles, vehicles of a word which judges and saves. That is what emerges from a study of the scheme used by the author in his message to each of the churches.

The scheme consists of six elements: the address or the recipient, the introduction of Christ, a word of judgment (positive and/or negative), a call for conversion or perseverance, an invitation to listen to the Spirit, and a promise.

The address is presented in a uniform way. Only the name of the church varies: 'To the angel of the church in X write . . .' The prophetic word always has a specific addressee, an individual or community: 'Thus says the Lord to the house of Israel . . .' (Amos 5.4); 'Hear the Word of the Lord, children of Israel . . .' (Hosea 4.1); 'Vision of Isaiah . . . concerning Judah and Jerusalem . . .' (Isaiah 2.1); 'The word of the Lord came to me, saying, "Go and proclaim in the hearing of Jerusalem"' (Jeremiah 2.1–2). More often than not it is the community, the people of God, who is addressed. In the case of the seven churches, the immediate recipient is the 'angel of the church', which here must be taken as a personification of the particular church.

Then comes the introduction of Christ (one could really say that he introduces himself): 'The words of . . .' Such a formula is evidently copied from the prophetic oracles of the Old Testament introduced by the formula 'Thus says the Lord' and its numerous variants. Beyond the individual and very rich titles revealed to each of the churches, Christ appears essentially as the Word of God, who addresses all the churches.

The third element is defined differently by the commentators. Here I have kept the word judgment simply because of its ambiguity; the judgment of the works of each of the churches can be positive or negative, or both at once. A double formula introduces the judgment, 'I know your conduct . . .' and 'But I have this against you . . .' Now this recalls the numerous prophetic pleas (sometimes called Yahweh's cause with his people) denouncing the infidelity of the people of God. However, we should note that the praise of the communities is a new development from the prophetic oracles. Certainly, there is no lack of promises of restoration and happiness for the people among the prophets, but

there seems to be no such thing as a congratulatory oracle.

After the judgment necessarily comes the call to conversion ('Repent') in the case of a faulty and defective church, or the call for perseverance ('Stand fast . . . be faithful . . . do not fear') in the case of a church to which Christ does not address any reproach. Here again John is to be included among the host of prophets who, having denounced the inertia, the injustice, the ingratitude and the infidelities of the people, always keep hoping for their conversion and return to the covenant: 'Wash yourselves; make yourselves clean; remove the evil of your doings from before my eyes; cease to do evil; learn to do good' (Isa. 1.16–17); 'Return, Israel, to Yahweh your God . . .' (Hosea 14.2); 'Return, O faithless sons, I will heal your faithlessness' (Jer. 3.22). Similarly, when Christ invites one or other of the churches to drive out fear and to stand firm, he takes up the innumerable words of consolation and hope uttered by the prophets above the crises experienced by the people.

The invitation to hear the Spirit, which appears as the penultimate element in the first three letters and then forms the conclusion of the four last letters, confirms their prophetic tenor. So it is Christ who has spoken and the Spirit who must be heard. This formula, very much in place as a conclusion, in a way serves as a signature to the prophetic oracles of Christ. The Christ who speaks is the Christ invested with the fullness of Spirit which inspired the prophets. And just as the prophets in their day ended a large number of the oracles with the formula 'oracle of the Lord' or 'word of the Lord', so the 'letters' end with a declaration which brings out the authority of the word of Christ while at the same time indicating the conditions on which this word could bear fruit: the churches have to listen to the Spirit.

Finally, the promise, in last or penultimate position, admirably matches the structure and the dynamics of the prophetic books. While the prophets multiply denunciations and calls to conversion, their books, as we have already seen, unfailingly end with the most splendid promises of salvation. Precisely because they are of prophetic inspiration, the proclamations to the churches can only end by the invocation of an unprecedented future, deriving directly from the power of the resurrection of Christ.

## Reality or fiction: the seven churches?

No one would dream of denying that the message addressed to the churches is prophetic and still topical. But there may still be a question whether the portrait which John traces of the churches is realistic, concrete and historical, or highly stylized and somewhat fictitious.

A first reading might suggest fiction, first of all by very reason of the figure seven and the stereotyped character of so many expressions. The concern to teach which so inspires John would, it might seem, lead him to present a situation which could be thought representative, hence the idea of the seven churches. And it is true that beyond the individual physiognomy of the churches, John delivers a message addressed to 'all the churches'. A second surprise which tells against realism is the omission of churches like Troas, Miletus and Colossae, which are well known elsewhere in the New Testament and belong to the same region as the churches of Apocalypse 2–3. And finally, at least for those who have some expertise in the ancient history and geography of Asia Minor, the direct light shed by these chapters on the local churches remains all in all very fragmentary and difficult to interpret. The text has little to offer to commentaries of a historical kind.

On the other hand, John addresses specific, well-characterized churches which are faced with quite particular problems. The choice of cities can easily be explained by the fact that they were all part of an imperial network of roads, served by courier. Another factor which may have guided John in his choice is emperor worship: all the cities mentioned, perhaps with the exception of Thyatira, bear witness to and have traces of the worship offered to the Roman emperor. And finally, even if they are not legion,

the allusions to the characteristics of some cities show that John had a good knowledge of the circles he was addressing: for example the 'crown' of Smyrna (connected with its fortifications and its games), the 'throne of Satan' in Pergamum (with its vast statue of Jupiter and its temple dedicated to Augustus), the 'new name' given to Philadelphia which had indeed changed its name under the emperor Tiberius, or finally the reputation of Laodicea for its pharmaceutical products (the famous 'collyrium' for the eyes) and textiles ('buy . . . white garments') and its financial exploits ('You say, I am rich, I have prospered, I need nothing . . .').

If the allusions are not always self-evident, it nevertheless remains a fact that John had quite specific communities in view, for the most part rich in a Christian life which they had already experienced, but also already threatened from outside and within and facing formidable challenges.

## A well-orchestrated crescendo . . .

We have already seen how John has made use of a pattern or model composed of six elements which are more or less uniform or variable in expression or content. But he has done more than that. By organizing chapters 2 and 3 in terms of seven, he has also sought to convey a message through the structure as a whole. A more careful examination of the box on page 70 will show that the churches on the list with uneven numbers have a negative balance sheet and consequently receive an unequivocal and imperative call to conversion. On the other hand, the balance sheet drawn up for the churches corresponding to the even numbers in the seven is clearly extremely positive. So we should not be surprised to see that they receive no call to conversion. The case of Thyatira is rather more complex, but it remains the case that the church of Thyatira itself does not receive any call to conversion: it is rather to Jezebel that the call is addressed.

One could cite in detail the links which join, for

73

example, churches 1 and 3, 2 and 6, and 5 and 7. However, it should be enough to note the crescendo, in the case of the even numbers, in the assertions of infidelity, ending up in the severest judgment for Laodicea, and the affirmations of steadfastness and fidelity in the case of the even numbers. This progression, and the specific position of the fourth church, Thyatira, could be represented by the following figure:

| 1 | 2 | 3 | 4 | 5 | 6 | 7 |
|---|---|---|---|---|---|---|
|  |  |  | 4 |  |  |  |
|  |  |  | Thyatira |  |  |  |
|  | 2 |  |  |  | 6 |  |
|  | Smyrna |  |  |  | Philadelphia |  |
| 1 |  | 3 |  | 5 |  | 7 |
| Ephesus |  | Pergamum |  | Sardes |  | Laodicea |

The singular position of Thyatira is quite amazing, all the more so since it is the least important and least renowned of the seven cities mentioned. However, despite its lack of renown, John seems to have wanted to confer special value on it: in a series of seven, there is no denying that it in effect occupies the central position. Is this pure coincidence, or can we find other indications to confirm this first observation?

A first confirmation comes in the length of the text. With its twelve verses, the message to Thyatira is the most developed (the others are six or seven verses on average). A second derives from the vocabulary used to describe the works of this church: 'I know your works, your love and faith and service and patient endurance, and that your latter works exceed the first' (2.19). Furthermore, the Greek sounds insistent, using the conjunction 'and' seven times. In the list, all that is lacking is the technical term for hope, but this is largely compensated for by that 'patient endurance'. So we have love (*agape*), faith, service (*diakonia*), hope-perseverance, and over and above this so many other works . . . As in the case of churches corresponding to an even number, no call for conversion is addressed directly to the church of Thyatira itself.

A third confirmation of the singular character of the proclamation to the church of Thyatira relates to a christological title which is unique in the Apocalypse and is perhaps the most exalted one for expressing the divinity of Christ. This is the title 'Son of God', which is also presupposed in the conclusion to the 'letter', with the allusion to 'power from my Father' (v. 28).

The fourth singular feature is the content and scope of the promise. This is by far the most universalist of the seven, since 2.26–27 speaks of 'power over the nations'. Almost all the others have an individual focus, whereas here the horizon opens up on the nations and on participation in the power of Christ.

The fifth and last confirmation of the unique position of the church of Thyatira is that here we have the only use in the whole of the book of the

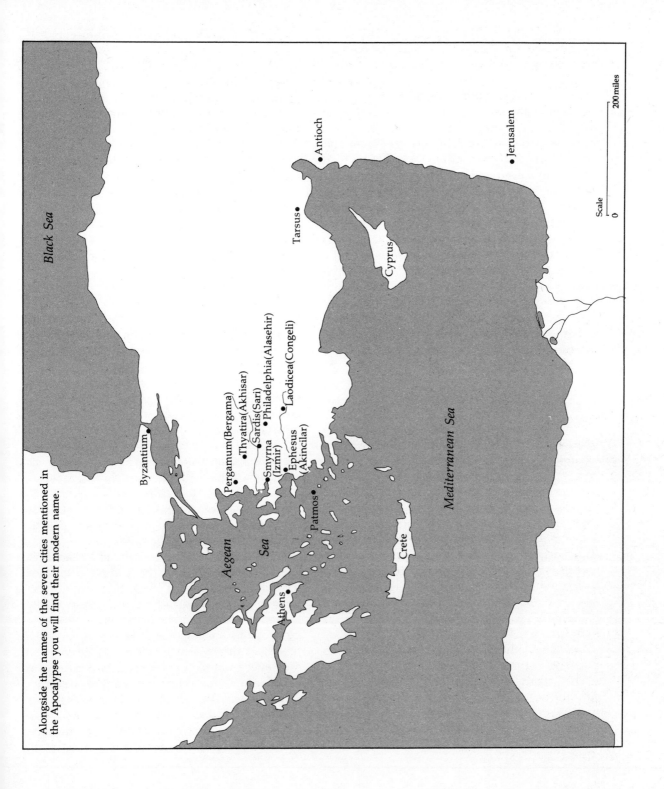

Alongside the names of the seven cities mentioned in
the Apocalypse you will find their modern name.

Black Sea

Byzantium •

Pergamum(Bergama) •
• Thyatira(Akhisar)
• Sardis(Sari)
• Philadelphia(Alasehir)
Smyrna • • Laodicea(Congeli)
(Izmir)
• Ephesus
(Akincilar)

Aegean
Sea

• Patmos

Athens •

Crete

Mediterranean Sea

Tarsus •

• Antioch

Cyprus

• Jerusalem

Scale

0

200miles

expression 'all the churches' (v. 23). This leads us directly to conclude that whereas the churches must already hear both the message addressed to them and that addressed to the other churches, John has made Thyatira a typical church. The message addressed to it has a more universal scope than the others. First of all, its works summarize the whole of Christian life. Secondly, the christological title which is unveiled to it takes us to the summit of New Testament christology. Thirdly, the promise links the one who conquers fully with the universal Lordship of Christ and his power to judge the nations. Fourthly, the long statement on Jezebel is beyond doubt a warning which applies to all the churches: it is important to know how to distinguish between true and false prophets and to resist the temptation to sacrifice to idols or to devote oneself to the 'deep things' of Satan, which promise a salvation which one can obtain by knowledge, without having practised works of justice and love.

## The history of salvation in miniature

The mastery which John shows of the great traditions of the Old Testament (mainly Genesis, Exodus, the prophets and the psalms) may well give extra importance to chapters 2–3. Recent authors, taking up a line of interpretation already present in the church fathers, suggest that one could have a prophetic and retrospective or recapitulatory reading of the 'letters' to the seven churches. Some details might seem forced, or to give rise to slightly different interpretations from those produced by a prophetic reading, but in the end the overall approach is quite convincing.

According to this type of reading, we would find here, in order, the main phases of the history of salvation in the Old Testament, right up to the threshold of the New Testament.

The promise to the church in Ephesus explicitly refers to 'the tree of life, which is in the paradise of God' (2.7), while the reproach addressed to it speaks of its fall and the loss of its first love. So this first stage would correspond to the story of Adam and Eve in paradise and the Fall.

The situation of the church in Smyrna is described in terms of tribulation and poverty (2.9); this corresponds to the condition of the Hebrew people in Egypt (Deut. 26.7). So perhaps we should understand the mention of the 'ten days of tribulation' as a veiled allusion to the ten plagues of Egypt, and the title of Christ referring to his death in the same way, since later in the book (11.8) John describes the city where the Lord was crucified as 'Sodom and Egypt'. If we accept these parallels, the message to the church in Smyrna would in turn evoke the time of the stay in Egypt and the deliverance brought by the exodus.

In the case of the church of Pergamum, one thinks spontaneously of the next stage, that of the time in the wilderness, since John refers directly to the 'hidden' manna and the figure of 'Balaam' which we find in the book of Numbers (chs. 22–24).

With Thyatira, we would find ourselves in the time of the monarchy. This is suggested on the one hand by the quotation of Ps. 2, which is so messianic and so bound up with the figure of David, and is completed with an allusion to the morning star also interpreted in messianic terms, and on the other with the mention of Jezebel.

As for Sardis, the author tells us that only 'some' have been found faithful; this suggests the 'remnant' which is so often mentioned by the prophets at the time of the exile.

The promise to the church in Philadelphia speaks of the 'pillar of the Temple', the 'new Jerusalem'; this brings us to the time of reconstruction on the return from exile. And finally, for some interpreters the extremely severe judgment made on the church of Laodicea would represent the extreme crisis of the time of the Maccabees, or for others the situation of the crisis of Judaism against which Jesus has to be seen.

In this way the prophecy of Apocalypse 2–3 becomes a parable: on the one hand it addresses the church contemporary with John and continues to be topical for the churches to come, and on the other it indicates the awareness the primitive church had of reliving the major stages of the history of salvation already presented in the Old Testament and fulfilled in an unprecedented and definitive way in the resurrection of Christ.

### In short . . .

Let us now recall the essentials of the message of Apocalypse 2–3.

1. The christological dimension, so strong throughout the book, here reaches unparalleled heights. Here, as everywhere else in the Apocalypse, we find the Christ of the paschal mystery, glorious and exalted in his death and resurrection. Furthermore, here more than anywhere else in the book John presents us with a Christ who is present in his church and Lord of his church: he knows it, praises it and censures it, exhorts it vigorously to be converted or to be faithful, and promises it a part in his victory. It is also in these two chapters that Christ appears more as the 'Word of God' through his principal activity, which is to speak to the churches in prophetic fashion, himself being invested with the fullness of the Spirit which inspires the prophets. And finally, John presents us with a Christ who is equal to God, claiming for him titles which the Old Testament keeps for God alone: Holy, Amen, First and Last, Living One.

2. These two chapters undeniably have a liturgical dimension. On the one hand the coming of Christ plays an important role here (it is mentioned six times). Now the conclusion of the book with its 'Maranatha. Come, Lord Jesus', shows us that the hope of the coming of the Lord finds its chief place of expression in the framework of the liturgy. On the other hand, the themes of the new creation, the white garments, the crown of life and the hidden manna unfailingly remind Christians of baptism and the eucharist.

3. By their very sobriety, the 'letters' show the main problems and challenges facing the different churches. Here, just under the surface, we find the two main problems of relations with Judaism (who are the true Jews?) and Roman emperor worship ('the throne of Satan'), and the backdrop is that of trial, tribulation and martyrdom. Toleration of and compromise with idolatry and gnosis are also among the temptations which threaten the communities addressed by John. But whatever the problem envisaged, the word of Christ is always the same: there is a need for conversion and a return to the most radical demands of the Gospel, to the original fervour.

4. Finally, as I have already emphasized elsewhere, the promises made to the churches show us that the benefits traditionally expected at the end of time are already accessible to 'those who conquer', thanks to the resurrection of Christ. For example, access to the tree of life and the hidden manna that the Jews hope for at the end of time is made possible now for anyone who undertakes to follow Christ in his mystery of death-and-resurrection. This is certainly the good news that the 'letters' bring to churches asking themselves about the tribulations they have been through and the delays which seem to be involved in the return of Christ. There is nothing evident about this good news; it must be understood with the help of the spirit: 'He who has an ear, let him hear what the Spirit says to the churches' (2.7).

# 7

# 'The Lamb Standing as Though it had been Slain', or the True Face of God

### (Apocalypse 4–5)

The appearance of a 'Lamb as though it had been slain', which is nevertheless standing, is without doubt one of the most unexpected and dramatic features of the Apocalypse. It is unexpected, because here we have the first use of the word and the image of the Lamb (which will occur another twenty-eight times), and dramatic, since the chapter opens on an impasse: the book held by God is 'sealed with seven seals' (5.1), and John is in tears on learning that 'no one in heaven or on earth or under the earth was able to open the scroll or to look into it' (5.3). However, the tension is quickly broken when one of the elders declares, 'Weep not; lo, the Lion of the tribe of Judah, the Root of David, has conquered, so that he can open the scroll and its seven seals' (5.5). There is no doubt that this is a turning point in the book and a vision which determines the unfolding of what 'must take place after this' (4.1).

We can easily understand why the liturgy contains the whole of this chapter, both in the cycle of readings for the eucharistic liturgy and in the canticles for the offices. Nor is it surprising that Christian iconography should have this as one of its favourite themes.

However, if we are to understand chapter 5 and its role in the Apocalypse properly, it is quite vital for us to connect it with its immediate context, chapter 4, which is strictly symmetrical and complementary to it. Read by itself, chapter 5 attributes a universal power of revelation to the Lamb, since it is he and he alone who is to 'open the seals', and the whole scene is equivalent to an enthronement liturgy, since the Lamb is called to share God's throne and is given the royal and judicial prerogatives which flow from this. This scene is all the more eloquent since it extends and deepens the vision of chapter 4.

## Two inseparable chapters

As with the message to the seven churches, we should note that chapters 4–5 are extremely well constructed and unified.

First of all we should note how the description of the two visions begins in the same way and from the start relates to the same object, 'one seated on the throne' (5.7, 9–10 and above all 5.13), who is certainly the dominant figure in the vision of chapter 4. So the aim of chapter 5 is to tell us what are the links between God and the Lamb. These links already appear in the fact that the Lamb 'took the scroll from the right hand of him who was seated on the throne' (5.7), and they emerge even more strikingly in the three doxologies of ch. 5, which are manifestly modelled on the doxology of 4.11: 'You are worthy, our Lord and God, *to receive glory and honour and power, for* you created all things, and by your will they are and were created' (the words in italic are taken up in the doxologies to the Lamb in chapter 5). Finally, the links are so close that the final doxology addresses both the Lamb and him who sits on the throne (5.13).

Two other unifying factors should be added to this first one. On the one hand, everything takes place around the throne (nineteen of the forty-four uses of the word in the Apocalypse occur in these two chapters). Here we truly have an enthronement scene and the recognition of a royal dignity. On the other hand, the secondary figures are the same, namely 'the four living creatures' and the 'twenty-four elders', whose role is chiefly liturgical: they prostrate themselves in worship, they sing and proclaim, and their mission is to present 'the prayers of the saints'. We shall have to come back to the identity of these figures later. For the moment let us simply note how their presence also contributes to the unity of chapters 4–5.

While there is unity, we must also note the meaning that emerges from such a coherence. Chapters 4 and 5 turn on fundamental theological questions. The first is the possibility of seeing God: if God shows himself, where and how can he be recognized? The second is the understanding of the scriptures, here seen as the Old Testament (the sealed book): what has this book to say if one is a disciple of the Lamb and a reader of the Gospels? These are very serious questions, but are treated extraordinarily well by John, who once again gives us an extremely powerful and original synthesis.

## 'See God . . . and live' (chapter 4)

For the patriarchs of the Old Testament, here represented by the twenty-four elders (see below on their identity), the mystery of God was so great and impressive that they had come to the conclusion that one simply could not see God and live. The face of God had to remain hidden; at the most, they thought, God could show his 'back': 'You cannot see my face; for man shall not see me and live' (Ex. 33.20). People were so convinced of this that the mere idea of having transgressed such a prohibition evoked nothing less than terror. At Bethel, Jacob shudders at having encountered God, though only in a dream, and exclaims, 'How awesome is this place!' (Gen. 28.17). And after struggling with God himself on the banks of the river Jabbok, he is utterly surprised to be still alive: 'So Jacob called this place Peniel, saying, "For I have seen God face to face, and yet my life is preserved"' (Gen. 32.31). Samson's parents have the same kind of reaction: 'We shall surely die,' Manoah says to his wife, 'for we have seen God' (Judg. 13.22).

We might say that here was a kind of popular prejudice, which was very strong, that access to God should remain difficult, if not downright impossible. However, the reality is more complex, and we have to say that already in the Old Testament God did everything possible to reverse this prejudice. Furthermore, it is significant that in none of the cases quoted in the previous paragraph did anyone die! On the contrary. And as far as Moses is concerned, does not the same book of Exodus say that 'Yahweh used to speak to Moses face to face, as a man speaks to his friend' (Ex. 33.11)?

It is in this two-fold context that Apocalypse 4 has to be understood. Certainly God appears here as the one who is wholly other, holy and transcendent, and has to be recognized as such. But at the same time God takes numerous initiatives in making himself known and revealing his true face.

Here again, John shows a remarkable talent, bordering on genius. He has in fact been able to bring together in one chapter the four greatest theophanies of the Old Testament: at the burning bush (Ex. 3), on Sinai (Ex. 19–24), at the Temple of Jerusalem in the call of Isaiah (Isa. 6), and in Babylon 'by the river Chebar' in the call of

Ezekiel (Ezek. 1). So in the very short space of eleven verses in chapter 4, John takes us back to four major Old Testament texts which have played a tremendous part in the Jewish mystical tradition. By superimposing them or including one of them in another, John gives us something of the essentials and the best of what the Jewish tradition shows us about the mystery of God.

The first words which relate the vision begin by putting us in the context of a theophany: 'After this I looked, and lo, in heaven an open door!' (4.1). Not all of heaven is opened, but nevertheless here is an entrance into the heavenly and divine world. Then we immedi-ately encounter the experience of Moses on Sinai when in the very same verse John relates the words, 'Come up hither, and I will show you what must take place after this . . .' We cannot in fact help thinking of Moses receiving the order to climb Mount Sinai (Ex. 24.1–12). So a few verses later it is no surprise to hear John speaking of 'flashes of lightning and voices and peals of thunder' (4.5) which also marked the experience on Sinai (Ex. 19.16–19), and the 'seven torches of fire' burning before the throne (4.5) which in turn recall the 'devouring fire' of the glory of Yahweh (Ex. 24.17). The one who sits upon the throne is indeed the God of the Exodus.

# Re-experiencing the Exodus

John is very much inspired by the prophets. Nor did he fail to meditate on *the* experience of salvation in the Old Testament, the Exodus. In borrowing expressions or images from the biblical book of Exodus John already gives us his reading of contemporary history. For him, the death-and-resurrection of Christ is the event of decisive salvation, which brings humankind from slavery to freedom. Here is a reminder of the main recollections of the Exodus which run through the Apocalypse:

- 1.6: '(To him) . . . who has made us a kingdom, priests to his God and Father . . .' is inspired by Exodus 19.6;

- 1.8: The presentation of God as 'who is and who was and who is to come' is an original commentary on Exodus 3.14, which is without doubt the most important revelation of the divine name in the OT;

- 2.17: the gift of hidden *manna* is promised to the conqueror (cf. Ex. 16);

- 5.6: the slain Lamb achieves the victory prefigured by the offering of the paschal lamb;

- the mention of lightning, thunder and earthquakes is also part of the signs which accompanied the revelation of God on Sinai (Ex. 19.16);

- chapter 8 and 6: the seven trumpets and bowls take up a large proportion of the plagues of Egypt (Ex. 7–11);

- 11.8: the mention of Egypt in the author's own words is symbolic, and is given negative connotations: memories of the slavery and oppression inflicted on the people of God (Ex. 1);

- 15.1: those who conquer the Beast sing 'the Song of Moses' and also celebrate the mighty acts of God who frees his people from the oppressor (cf. Ex. 15).

That is made even clearer by the fact that the acclamation in v. 8 ends with a commentary which plays on the significance of the name Yahweh, revealed to (and at the same time veiled from) Moses in the episode of the burning bush. In revealing his name to Moses, God is in effect playing on the sense of the word Yahweh in Hebrew and its relations with the root which denotes 'being'. In Exodus 3.14 this verb is used twice, in a tense which is called unfinished and which could also be translated by an imperfect: 'I will be who I will be'. So when the four living creatures add to their 'Holy, holy, holy' the acclamation 'who was and is and is to come', in a way they give us a commentary on the life and the movement which exist in God. The God of Moses and the Exodus is a God who is involved in the future of history and who cannot be reduced to a static and abstract definition. He is the God who 'is before', the God who comes from the future.

From the God of Moses we pass easily to the God of the prophets, represented here by the one who has been called 'the prince of the prophets', Isaiah. His calling and his message derive completely from his experience of God: a holy, transcendent and omnipotent God. By taking up in verse 8 the very words of Isaiah's vision, 'Holy, holy, holy, is the Lord God almighty', Isaiah also presents us with a God of majesty, the Wholly Other and the All-Powerful, the master of creation.

And finally, this chapter is even more marked by the influence of Ezekiel, with the mention and the description of the four living creatures (4.6–8), and his representation of the glory of the 'one seated on a throne' (4.2). More than one feature of this figure is borrowed from the vision of the 'chariot' and the glory of Yahweh with which Ezekiel was favoured 'on the banks of the river Chebar' (Ezek. 1.1) at the time of the deportation to Babylon.

So as in the case of the messages to the 'seven churches', John gives us a panoramic vision of the great moments of the revelation of God in the Old Testament, and does so with the aim of preparing his readers better for the full and definitive vision of God in the figure of the Lamb (chapter 5).

## The true face of God: a lamb 'standing as though it had been slain' (chapter 5)

Having given us a real symphony of Old Testament theophanies, John now brings us to a 'christophany' (a manifestation of Christ): 'And between the throne and the four living creatures and among the elders, I saw a Lamb standing, as though it had been slain, with seven horns and seven eyes, which are the seven spirits of God sent out into all the earth' (5.6). This is the climax to which John wanted to bring us and from which he invites us to contemplate the true face of God.

One could not imagine a more gripping contrast. After the images of majesty in chapter 4, here we are brought to the great paradox of the gospel: that of a humble and suffering Messiah who has chosen to go through suffering and death ('a Lamb, as though it had been slain'), but recognized and exalted by God to such a degree that he is 'standing' and bears the insignia of royalty and divinity ('seven horns and seven eyes, which are the seven Spirits of God').

Christian faith will never finish meditating on a page like Apocalypse 5, which expresses so well the scandal and the glory of the cross of Christ. In the form of imagery, and quite boldly, John brings us to the heart of the paschal experience and the newness of the gospel. The God of the Christians is not the immovable God of the philosophers nor a God who has chosen to live in an ivory tower without ever having been compromised by history. On the contrary, God is to be discovered at the heart of history and human suffering as the one who has no fear of serving suffering humanity and transforming suffering through his own love. For it is not suffering that has saved the world but the love of God and Christ for the world (cf. John 3.16–17; 13.1).

Faithful to the tradition of the Gospels (above all the passion narratives) and the original missionary proclamation (see e.g. Acts 2; 4; 10; 13),

John shows great sobriety in his presentation of the slain Lamb and does not play on any sentiments. His intention is theological, and he celebrates the victory of Christ to the utmost. However, it can never be forgotten that the Lamb is worthy and standing precisely because he has fully and courageously accepted a destiny which implied suffering.

So we must revise our image of God, and from now on the vision of the Lamb 'as though slain' and 'standing' is, for us Christians, the one that best expresses the mystery of the God in whom we believe.

### Where does the Christian part begin?

A first reading of chapters 4 and 5 has already brought out an important contrast. Whereas chapter 4 is saturated with quotations from the Old Testament and takes up themes which are dear to biblical and extra-biblical Judaism, chapter 5 has a completely Christian accent with the appearance of the figure of the Lamb (= Christ), whose victory it celebrates with solemnity and to whom it exclusively attributes the power to open the sealed book.

But is the contrast so pronounced at this point that we have to follow some commentators in saying that chapter 4 is a chapter which reflects only Jewish traditions and is totally lacking in any Christian reference? Were that the case, then chapter 4 as a whole would be marginal and badly positioned, particularly between chapters 2–3 and 5, the Christian content of which is so dense. Perhaps there is meant to be a contrast! But there is also a symmetry, which suggests complementarity, and it has to be acknowledged that chapter 4 is quite in place in a Christian apocalypse.

The strictly Christian character of chapter 4 is above all connected with two elements. The first is the key element: there is 'the first voice, which I had heard speaking to me like a trumpet' (4.1) and which is that of the 'son of man' of the inaugural vision (cf. 1.10–13). In other words,

the vision of chapter 4, like the messages to the seven churches (2–3), comes in the wake of the initial christological vision. Just as discreetly, the presence of Christ the 'son of man' already allows decisive light to be shed on the main manifestations of God in the Old Testament.

So Christ is not absent from chapter 4, nor are the Christians. Indeed, even if the 'twenty-four elders' represent figures from the Old Testament, we must not forget, first, that the term 'elder' remained significant for Christians, and secondly, that these elders are described with the same attributes as the Christians, since they are 'clad in white garments, with golden crowns upon their heads' (4.4; cf. also 4.10), and they have been provided with 'twenty-four thrones around the throne' (4.4). In other words, the resurrection of Christ enables the elders to share in the promises made to the churches (3.5, 11, 21). There is an unbroken continuity between the elders and the Christians who have remained faithful to the Lamb.

### From the mystery of the twenty-four elders . . .

Once the general sense of chapters 4–5 has been established, we can return to the two enigmas posed by the text: who are the twenty-four elders and what is their role? And what can be this 'scroll written within and on the back, sealed with seven seals'?

The twenty-four elders, or at least one of them, are mentioned twelve times in all in the Apocalypse (4.4, 11; 5.5, 8, 9–10; 7.13; 11.16, 17–18; 19.4). Their main role is liturgical: prostration, adoration, praise and intercession. On two occasions only one of them plays the role of interpreter for John (5.5; 7.13). Although they are associated with the figure of the four living creatures and in concert with a 'multitude of angels', it is never said that they participate in the divine council and the government of the world.

We can reduce to three the questions raised about their identity in the history of Christian exegesis: 1. Are these angels or human beings? 2. If they are human beings, are they figures of the Old Testament or the New? 3. Why the number twenty-four?

The answer to the first question seems clear: these are human beings and not angels. Why? First of all because the name 'elders' (*presbyteroi* in Greek) is never used in the Bible for angels, whereas it is a technical term for speaking of the spiritual heads of Israel, old or new. One cannot see why John should have departed from this usage. And secondly, whereas throughout the Jewish tradition, biblical or extrabiblical, angels certainly form the heavenly court and surround the divine throne, there is no text which makes them 'sit upon thrones' or wear 'crowns'. This privilege is accorded only to believers. So, both in their title and their attributes, the twenty-four elders cannot be angelic beings; they belong to the world of believers.

However, the second question remains: are they believers of the first covenant or the new covenant, or perhaps both at once? In other words, are these patriarchs or saints of the Old and New Testaments, patriarchs and apostles? In fact the answer to this question is itself bound up with the interpretation of the figure twenty-four.

One suggestion based on the comparative study of religions would have John influenced by the Babylonian tradition of a pantheon of twenty-four star-gods. This is not impossible as a secondary derivation, but the best explanation still remains with the Old Testament and Jewish traditions. There are then two possibilities.

The first possibility is offered by I Chronicles. In fact according to I Chronicles 24–25 David ordered the service of the priests and singers who were to officiate in the Temple of Yahweh by classes of twenty-four. A second possible explanation comes to us from an ancient Jewish tradition according to which the Bible consisted of twenty-four books. We can find the echo of such a tradition at the end of IV Esdras, that non-canonical Jewish apocalypse, slightly later than the texts of John, but clearly conveying traditions which were well-established in Judaism. For 'forty days' the scribe Esdras speaks in abundance under the impact of divine inspiration, while five men 'trained to write rapidly' take down what he says. The result is that 'in forty days ninety-four books were written. And when the forty days were ended, the Most High spoke to me, saying, "Make public the twenty-four books that you wrote first and let the worthy and the unworthy read them; but keep the seventy that were written last, in order to give them to the wise among your people"' (IV Esdras 14.44–46).

The figure 'seventy', which is of course symbolic, here denotes the apocalyptic literature which is considered esoteric and reserved for an elite of 'the wise'. That leaves twenty-four books which are to be published for all, worthy and unworthy. These are the twenty-four books that Judaism traditionally holds sacred. Other authors, like Flavius Josephus, reduce the number to twenty-two, but twenty-four remains the best attested.

So these two traditions lead us to see the 'twenty-four elders' as Old Testament figures, perhaps priests and temple singers, perhaps biblical writers. Do we have to choose between these two traditions? It is not unthinkable that John wanted to fuse them, and both fit very well with the context of Apocalypse 4–5. The clearly liturgical dimension of these two chapters corresponds at every point to the preoccupations of the Chronicler, and the role of the 'twenty-four elders' is very close to that of the temple singers. On the other hand, since chapter 5 speaks of a book which, as we shall very soon see, represents the Old Testament, it is not surprising that John should have appealed to this other Jewish tradition: not only the theophanic texts but the whole of the Old Testament writings point in the direction of the Lamb.

### . . . to the mystery of the sealed book

Alongside the figure of the twenty-four elders, the image of the 'scroll written within and on the back, sealed with seven seals' presents itself as one of the most important enigmas of chapters 4–5.

We cannot rule out the possibility of seeing, with all of apocalyptic, a book of 'secrets' concerning the destinies of the world and of individuals, since this opening of the seals (chapter 6 and 7) offers a prophetic reading of the events of history, in a way unveiling truths which have hitherto been kept secret. It could also be the book of life, which is mentioned several times in the Apocalypse itself (3.5; 13.8; 17.8; 20.15; 21.27).

One thing is certain: this is the book of the Word of God. For it is God who holds it 'in his right hand' (5.1) and it is from God that the Lamb is to take it (5.7–8). In other words, the book has its source in God, and what will be unveiled by the Lamb is based on the very authority of God ('his right hand'). On the other hand, we must not forget that John borrows the image of the book (which is not necessarily the same as the 'little scroll' in chapter 10) from the prophet Ezekiel: 'And when I looked, behold, a hand was stretched out to me, and lo, a written scroll was in it; and he spread it before me; and it had writing on the front and on the back, and there were written on its words of lamentation and mourning and woe' (Ezek. 2.9–10). In the case of the prophet Ezekiel, it is clearly the word of God that he has to proclaim to his people.

Can we be more specific about the book opened by the Lamb, and which also represents the Word of God? It seems to me that the immediate context of the Apocalypse and the wider content of the New Testament invites us to see this as the Old Testament. We have rightly seen that chapter 4 is steeped in the Old Testament and that the figure of the twenty-four elders can be related to that of the twenty-four writers of the Old Testament books. Furthermore, it is easy to see this scene as the dramatization of a major

theological standpoint of the New Testament writers, and especially the evangelists: the scriptures can only be understood in the light of the event of Jesus Christ. So it is that among the four evangelists we find a clear expression of the conviction that Jesus fulfils the scriptures. This standpoint is very well illustrated by the scene on the Emmaus road: 'And beginning with Moses and all the prophets, he interpreted to them in all the scriptures the things concerning himself' (Luke 24.27). John of the Apocalypse says nothing different: it is the Lamb 'standing as though it had been slain', i.e. the dead and risen Christ, who alone allows us to understand the whole of the scriptures.

### A model of liturgy

While the liturgical dimension is omnipresent in the Apocalypse, beyond question chapters 4 and 5 are the chapters in which it achieves its most perfect expression. First of all in the vocabulary, which is particularly rich in terms with a liturgical resonance. First there are the instruments: we have the trumpet (4.1) announcing the sacred assemblies (Lev. 23; 24; 25.9; cf. also Num. 10.1–10) and the harp (5.8), instruments which are so often associated with the Old Testament psalms and canticles. So we are not surprised to learn that the living creatures and the elders are to sing 'a new song' (5.9). Secondly, the mention of the 'golden bowls full of incense' (5.8) puts us first of all in the context of the liturgies of the sanctuary (Ex. 30). Thirdly, we find a highly representative range of biblical terms connected with prayer: 'be in the Spirit' (4.2), offer 'glory, honour and thanks' (4.9), 'fall down' and 'worship' (4.10; 5.8, 14), 'sing' (5.9), 'the prayers of the saints' (5.8). Fourthly, we find ourselves in the thick of liturgy, with no less than five doxologies (occupying six of the twenty-five verses that make up these two chapters), rich in the accents of the hymnic prayer of the Old Testament, and punctuated with the well-known refrains of the prayer of the psalms, 'for ever and ever' (4.9–10; 5.13) and 'amen' (5.14).

We should have no illusions about the provenance of such liturgical practices. They reflect the concrete practice of the synagogues and the young Christian churches. But they also serve as models and aim to give a complete vision of Christian prayer which must affirm both the omnipotence and holiness of the creator God and the universality of the salvation earned by the Lamb.

## A masterful opening

In a number of respects, chapters 4 and 5 differ from the rest of the Apocalypse. This is on the one hand because their framework is exclusively heavenly (perhaps with the exception of 5.10), and on the other because they do not form part of any of the series of seven around which the book is organized: letters to the seven churches (2–3), seven seals (6–7), seven trumpets (8–9) and seven bowls (15–16).

But here again we have to note that John has a happy touch and that he has used these two chapters to announce the themes to come. Thus, for example, the mention of the 'seven seals' in 5.1, 5 refers to the action of chapters 6–7, which consist in the opening of each of the seals. Similarly, the symbolism of the book is not exclusive to chapter 5; it will be taken up in chapter 10. So these two chapters have to be read in parallel. Another extremely important piece of symbolism for the book as a whole is that connected with the 'throne', which is sometimes understood as a throne of judgment and sometimes as a royal throne. Briefly evoked in 2.13, this symbolism is to play a very major role in chapter 13, which will be concerned with the

claims of the Beast to royal domination. By presenting his heavenly liturgy in honour of 'him who sits upon the throne' and the Lamb, John demystifies in advance the blasphemous enterprise of the Beast (13.4). His description of the Lamb with the 'seven horns' celebrates the fullness of the power gained and the salvation achieved by Christ (5.9–12), in contrast to the universal domination of the Beast (13.7–8).

Chapter 15, which is only eight verses long, borrows an impressive number of elements from the vision in chapters 4–5: the crystal sea (v. 2), the harps and the song (2–3), a doxology (3–4), the four living creatures and the God who lives for ever and ever (v. 7), and finally the theophany or manifestation of the glory of God (v. 8). The same has to be said of chapter 19, which is also very close to the theophanies of chapters 4–5, and which refers to the same figures: 'He who sits upon the throne', 'the four living creatures' and the 'twenty-four elders'.

Finally, in the description of the new Jerusalem we find once again three of the precious stones mentioned in 4.3: jasper, cornelian and emerald (cf. 21.19–20). The liturgy which is unfolded in chapters 4–5 gives us a foretaste of the one which will unfold in the new Jerusalem, where, however, there will no longer be any reason for the liturgical mediations of the present day: 'And I saw no temple in the city, for its temple is the Lord God the Almighty and the Lamb' (21.22).

There are so many links with the other sections of the book that we have to recognize that chapters 4–5 are very much in place where they are. John cannot find a better scenario with which to open his great prophetic fresco about 'what must take place after this' (6–22).

# 8

# From Judgment to Salvation

**(Apocalypse 6–7)**

## A turning point

With chapters 6–7 (completed by the first verse of chapter 8) we enter on a new literary scheme which is so well woven that it will take us right up to chapter 22. In fact, here we see the appearance of a first series specifically numbered from one to seven, a successive development with increasing dramatic intensity and a clearly universalistic scope. Strictly speaking, the Apocalypse has three such series: the seven seals (6.1–8.1), the seven trumpets (8.2–11.19) and the seven bowls (15.5–16.21). These three series of seven have so many verbal, thematic and structural affinities that we need only look at one of them to be able to interpret them all correctly. In fact, since each of them has a prelude and an extension, one could say that the whole architecture of the book from chapter 4 to chapter 22 is based on them. However, before demonstrating this linkage up to chapter 22, let us look at the main parallels between these three literary complexes and then consider the first of the three, which is without doubt the most famous, with the four riders and the number 144,000.

## The fate of humanity

As I have already said, John is interested in the events which have marked the existence of the Christian communities over the several decades prior to the composition of his book. But his preoccupations go well beyond the circle of the Christian communities. Starting from the experience of the first communities, John offers us a reflection on the fate of humanity generally. The consequences and the fruits of the resurrection of Christ extend to the whole of humanity. So we shall not be surprised to see that the three series of seven have a clearly universal scope. Simply from the author's use of sequences of seven we can understand, according to the biblical symbolism, that he is seeking to deliver a message addressed to humanity as a whole, one which unveils the full meaning of the course of history. Over and above this numerical procedure, in each of the series John also gives us more specific indications of the universality of the phenomena which he describes.

In the case of the seven seals, the mention of the four living creatures, the four riders (6.1–8) and the 'four angels standing at the four corners of the earth' (7.1) shows us clearly that what is happening concerns the whole of humanity. As for the trumpets, here again we find a mention of the 'four angels' (9.14–15) who have power over all the inhabited earth. This is further confirmed by the 'loud voice' of the great eagle: 'Woe, woe, woe to those who dwell on the earth . . .' (8.13). But it is not only the announcements of disaster which concern the whole of humanity. Each time the victory of God and of the Lamb is proclaimed within this series of seven, John stresses the extent of their power. So he speaks of 'him who lives for ever and ever, who created heaven and what is in it, the earth and what is in it, and the sea and what is in it . . .' (10.6) and celebrates the advent of the kingdom of God: 'The kingdom of this world has become the kingdom of our Lord and of his Christ; and he shall reign for ever and ever' (11.15). The God who is at work in the world is the 'Lord God almighty' (11.17). Finally, unlike the first two series of seven, the scourges spurred by the 'seven bowls of the wrath of God' (16.1) have a considerable impact, affecting whole sectors. For example, not only is 'a third of the sea' turned to blood, but the entire sea 'died and every living thing died that was in the sea' (16.3). The following verse speaks of the same fate reserved for the rivers and fountains of water, considered globally. And as for those affected by the different scourges, John speaks of 'men' (16.8–9, 11, 17, 21) without further distinction.

### 'The end has come!'

A second feature common to the series of seven is that they have an eschatological scope: again, we must understand this word 'eschatological' properly. Let us remember that John is giving a reading of past events which are well rooted in history. But his reading stems from his belief in the resurrection of Christ, which he sees as *the* eschatological event. Where other New Testament authors (like John the Evangelist) see eschatology already realized in the beginning of the ministry of Jesus, the John of the Apocalypse considers that it is the resurrection of Christ which marks the end of a world and inaugurates the definitive world willed by God.

Now contrary to what one might expect, John does not speak of the advent of this world only at the end of his work (in chapters 21 and 22), but right through his book. And it is striking that the end is evoked in each of the three series of seven. In fact the description of the sixth seal is steeped

in the vocabulary of 21–22 and already anticipates the glorious state of the inhabitants of the new Jerusalem:

$7^{15}$ *Therefore are they before the throne of God, and serve him day and night within his temple, and he who sits upon the throne will shelter them with his presence.* $^{16}$ *They shall hunger no more, neither thirst any more; the sun shall not strike them, nor any scorching heat.* $^{17}$ *For the Lamb in the midst of the throne will be their shepherd, and he will guide them to springs of living water; and God will wipe away every tear from their eyes.*

The second series of seven, the bowls, contains two references to the end. In 10.5–7 the angel speaks of the fulfilment of the mystery of God, and in 11.15–17 the twenty-four elders proclaim with great solemnity that the kingdom of God has finally come about and the divine judgment has been exercised in its two-fold dimension of salvation and punishment:

$10^5$ *And the angel whom I saw standing on sea and land lifted up his right hand to heaven* $^6$ *and swore by him who lives for ever and ever, who created the heaven and what is in it, the earth and what is in it, the sea and what is in it, that there should be no more delay,* $^7$ *but that in the days of the trumpet call to be sounded by the seventh angel, the mystery of God, as he announced to his servants the prophets, should be fulfilled.*

$11^{15}$ *Then the seventh angel blew his trumpet, and there were loud voices in heaven, saying, 'The kingdom of this world has become the kingdom of our Lord and of his Christ; and he shall reign for ever and ever.'* $^{16}$ *And the twenty-four elders who sit on their thrones before God fell on their face and worshipped God, saying,* $^{17}$ *'We give you thanks, Lord God almighty, who are and were, that you have taken your great power and begun to reign.'*

The last series of seven also duly gives us a scenario of the end. 'Then I saw another portent in heaven, great and wonderful, seven angels with seven plagues, which are the last, for with them the wrath of God is ended' (15.1). The cry of the seventh angel pouring out the seventh cup could hardly be more explicit: 'A great voice came out of the temple, from the throne, saying "It is done!"' (16.17). The end has truly come, as is also suggested by the testimony of another angel: 'Put in your sickle and reap, for the hour to reap has come, for the harvest of the earth is fully ripe' (14.15). And chapters 17–20 certainly emphasize the magnitude of the defeat of Babylon and the Dragon, and above all the victory of Christ, taking us to the vision of chapters 21–22, which describe in sublime terms the end of 'the old world' (21.4) and the creation of 'the new universe' (21.59).

## But what end . . .? For wrath . . .?

As I have said, there are numerous thematic links between the three series of seven. The most important consists in the theme of judgment evoked not only generally but even more specifically, from the perspective of the wrath of God, or of vengeance.

The first series of seven has two explicit mentions of this theme. First of all, the martyrs for the Word of God call for the advent of divine justice with loud cries: 'O Sovereign Lord, holy and true, how long before you judge and avenge our blood on those who dwell on the earth?' (6.10). We then have a comment which is first of all made by the kings of the earth, one which strikes every heart: '. . . the great day of wrath has come, and who can stand before it?' (6.17).

In the second series, the author reserves his reflections on judgment for the seventh trumpet. They are condensed into a single verse, containing both the positive and the negative sides of judgment (recompense – perdition): 'The nations raged, but your wrath came, and the time for the dead to be judged, for rewarding your servants, the prophets and saints, and those who fear your name, both small and great, and for destroying the destroyers of the earth' (11.18).

It is with the third series of seven that the

## The Dynamics of Judgment and Salvation in Apocalypse 6–22

| | Seals | Trumpets | Bowls |
|---|---|---|---|
| Prelude (in heaven): anticipation of *salvation* | chs. 4–5 | 8.2–5 | 15.1–4 |
| Advance signs of the end (on earth): *disaster – judgment* | ch. 6 | 8.6–9.21 | 16.1–17 |
| Interlude: delay *Hope of salvation* | 7.1–8 after the sixth seal | 10.1–11.4 after the sixth trumpet | [16.15] after the sixth bowl |
| Final triumph: *salvation* | 7.9–17 | 11.15–19 | chs. 17–22 |

judgment envisaged under the sign of wrath, hatred and vengeance achieves its climax. In the prelude to the seven bowls, 'those who have triumphed over the Beast' conclude their song of liberation with the image of a God of 'vengeance': 'Who shall not fear and glorify your name? For you alone are holy. All nations shall come and worship you, for your judgments have been revealed' (15.4). Then, once the third bowl has been poured out, 'the angel of water' is merciless on those who have been chastized: '"You are just in these your judgments, you who are and were, O Holy One, for men have shed the blood of saints and prophets, and you have given them blood to drink. It is their due!" And I heard the altar cry, "Yea, Lord God the Almighty, true and just are your judgments"' (16.5–7). Finally, the seventh bowl ends with the destruction of Babylon (= Rome), interpreted as the overflowing of the wrath of God: 'The great city was split into three parts, and the cities of the nations fell; and God remembered the great Babylon, to make her drain the cup of the fury of his wrath' (16.19). This theme is reintroduced and developed at will in the following chapters: 'Then one of the seven angels who had the seven bowls came and said to me, "Come, I will show you the judgment of the great harlot who is seated upon many waters . . ."' (17.1).

So there is an important dimension here which cannot be ignored. Faithful to the biblical tradition, and in particular the prophetic tradition of the 'Day of the Lord', John recalls with extreme vigour the severity of the judgment reserved for anyone who has made a pact with the Beast. There is a real alternative, and a choice has to be made, either for the Beast or for the Lamb. On this choice depends the outcome of the judgment: it will be for wrath . . .

### . . . or for salvation?

So the three series of seven have an analogous structure which deploys the dynamic, indeed the dialectic, of judgment-salvation. In all three cases there is then a whole chapter (two in the case of

the trumpets) to describe the signs heralding the end: these are the chapters which announce the judgment. This is the part of the series which is usually remembered, and which has put so many people off reading the Apocalypse. I have just said that this element is to be take seriously. But the framework in which these advance signs are presented cannot be emphasized enough (see the remarks in this connection in Chapter 5, page 61, 'What about the disasters?'), and this is built on visions of salvation. From a structural point of view these occupy an even more important part of chapters 4–22, divided into three sections. The prelude to each of the series of seven gives us refrains and songs which already celebrate the victory of the Risen Christ, or in the case of the trumpets remind us of the importance of the intercession of the saints. Then, in the linking of seals, trumpets and bowls, there is always a pause. There is a delay, which enables us to see that the punishment will not gain the upper hand. In the case of the bowls, the delay is introduced in a subtler and briefer way, but nothing prevents the beatitude of 16.15 from being orientated more towards salvation. And beyond the scourges the author gives us the last word of history, which is left to God, and which is translated into exceptional and definitive manifestations of salvation: splendid and already complete in chapter 7, the vision of salvation is briefer but nevertheless evocative in 11.15–19 and is developed fully and magnificently in 17–22 (above all in 19–22).

### 'So who can stand . . .?'

John's picture of the end and the signs which herald it is presented to us, as in chapters 4 and 5, in two panels. The first (chapter 6) shows the severity of the divine judgment and the scourges which strike humankind, and is essentially about the manifestations of the divine wrath. The second is all light, and in contrast brings out the innumerable ramifications of the salvation achieved by the Lamb.

# The Enigma of the First Rider

*'And I saw, and behold, a white horse, and its rider had a bow; and a crown was given to him, and he went out conquering and to conquer'* (6.2).

This verse poses one of the greatest puzzles of the Book of the Apocalypse and has given rise to the most extreme interpretations: both Christ and the Antichrist have been seen in it, and between them all the intermediaries associated with one or other figure.

At first sight, it seems as though we should see a maleficent power here, since the three other riders are bearers of evil and the whole of the sequence of seven seals has predominantly negative connotations (with the exception of the sixth seal). Furthermore, the description of the activities of the rider refers to the bow, which can be seen as a weapon of war, and thus of devastation.

On the other hand, it is even more striking how far the first rider is dissociated from the three others:

- The summary in 6.8 recalls the devastating action of the three other riders, but completely ignores the first rider in this matter;

- As we have already seen, almost everywhere else the colour white is associated with the divine world and the resurrection. It is hard to see why the white rider should be an exception, and announce disaster;

- In fact, the activities attributed to the white rider, far from having tragic and murderous connotations, point in the direction of the resurrection and its fruits, since it is said of the rider that 'a crown was given to him, and he went out conquering and to conquer'. Indeed, in the Apocalypse the crown is always the sign of the triumph of the righteous or of good over evil. And while the verb conquer is sometimes applied to the Beast, it nevertheless remains *the* verb for denoting the resurrection of Christ and the participation of Christians in his resurrection (the 'conqueror' of the 'letters to the seven churches');

- It could well be that the white rider is the same as that of 19.11, called 'faithful' and 'true', whose identity is unveiled: he is the 'Word of God' (19.13);

- Here, as in the other sequences of seven (8.2–5; 15.5–8), we could have a prelude or an introduction which already gives us a glimpse of the final victory;

- And finally, it should be stressed that the christological interpretation goes right back into Christian antiquity.

In short, there are more arguments which prompt us to see the white rider as a bringer of good news, associated with the divine world and that of the resurrection of Christ (though the rider need not necessarily be Christ himself). But we cannot discount the arguments which tell in the opposite direction, since it is the specific concern of chs. 6–7 to show the two-fold dimension of divine judgment: disaster and punishment for some, happiness and salvation for others.

Under the surface of chapter 6 we can see a profile of the theme, so dear to the prophetic tradition of the Old Testament, of the 'Day of Yahweh', which some had interpreted too easily in a complacent way (cf. Amos 5.18–20). Because of this, the prophets had also to recall the terrible aspect of this day for anyone who had been unfaithful to the covenant (see this same passage in Amos, and Joel 1.1–2). So on the part of Yahweh this day would imply an element of 'wrath', and for the people an element of 'darkness'. That is the perspective of Apocalypse 6. The riders, at least the last three, sow war, famine and death, and there follows a series of devastating plagues which spread confusion and anxiety on the earth.

The dramatic intensity of chapter 6 reaches a climax in the last verse, when the seer utters a cry of helplessness: 'For the great day of their (God's and the Lamb's) wrath has come, and who can stand before it?' (6.17). The very way in which the question is put indicates that it will be difficult, if not impossible, to escape the wrath of the Lamb. This is the formidable question to which chapter 7 is going to give the answer. Where chapter 6 forecasts a sombre and destructive future, chapter 7 projects a blazing light on the innumerable multitudes who have been able to stand and who form the one people of God, brought together in the death-and-resurrection of Christ.

## One and the same innumerable multitude? (Apocalypse 7)

We already saw in Chapter 3 the symbolism of the number 144,000: it is an ideal representation of the people of God. But do we necessarily have to see the 'great multitude which no man could number' in 7.9 (mentioned again in 14.1–5) as a distinct group? At first sight, it looks as if the answer should be in the affirmative, as I indicated in the explanation of the 144,000 in Chapter 3. According to this interpretation, the 144,000 would be the old Israel, represented as a very large number, and the 'great multitude'

would denote the church 'of the Gentiles'.

But it is possible to see in this chapter, as in so many other chapters of the Apocalypse, the use of a double image to describe a single reality: 7.1–8 and 7.9–17 could then speak of the same people of God, seen from a different perspective. In both cases there is an innumerable multitude: 144,000 could very well be translated by the expression in 7.9, a 'great multitude which no man could number'. The difference does not lie in the number but in the perspective. The first panel of the picture gives us an ideal representation of the people of God still on earth, and undergoing trial, while the second panel puts us in the heavenly liturgy, where there is also an ideal representation of the people of God. But this is always one and the same people of God, who have come forth from the resurrection of Christ. Since the resurrection of Christ, there is in fact no longer any reason for the distinctions between the old Israel and the new Israel. The apostle Paul put this very well: 'For as many of you as were baptized into Christ have put on Christ. There is neither Jew nor Greek, there is neither slave nor free, there is neither male nor female; for you are all one in Christ Jesus' (Gal. 3.27–28).

### A singular list

John is of the same school, and for him it is the resurrection of Christ which brings together the unique and innumerable people of God. This conviction could well lie behind the way in which he retouches the list of the tribes of Israel mentioned in 7.1–8. This fact has long been recognized: from Genesis 35.22–26 down to the texts of the New Testament, the Bible contains about thirty lists of the twelve tribes of Israel and knows no less than eighteen different arrangements of these lists, but the list in the Apocalypse does not match any of them! John has chosen his own way, in order to be able to communicate better his vision of the people of God:

1. The fact that he puts Judah at the head of the list is quite naturally explained by the messianic connection of this tribe. Jesus, 'first born of

# Apocalypse 7.9–17 and the Feast of Tabernacles

The second part of chapter 7 contains a number of references to the Feast of Tabernacles (Booths), the autumn feast first connected with the harvest according to Exodus 23.16, and then given a theological and spiritual significance at the time of Leviticus: 'You shall dwell in booths for seven days; all that are native in Israel shall dwell in booths, that your generation may know that I made the people of Israel dwell in booths when I brought them out of the land of Egypt: I am Yahweh your God' (Lev. 23.42–43).

In Apocalypse 7.9–17 there are at least four elements which can be understood on the basis of the Feast of Tabernacles as it was practised in the first century of our era:

1.  The immense multitude of the saved carry 'palms in their hands', as was the custom for the procession of the Feast of Tabernacles;

2.  Psalm 118, with its famous 'Hosanna' in v. 25, was a reading for these festival days. The substance of this cry is taken up in 7.10: 'Salvation to our God';

3.  The water brought in procession from the pool of Siloah played an extremely important role in the liturgical unfolding of the feast at the temple in Jerusalem. Now Apocalypse 7.17 tells us: 'For the Lamb in the midst of the throne will be their shepherd, and he will guide them to streams of living water.' There will no longer be any need to draw water from Siloah, since the Lamb will take the initiative in 'leading to springs of living water'.

4.  As enjoined, the first activity of the Feast of Tabernacles was to set up a booth. Here again we see an important shift in that this time it is God who takes the initiative: 'He who sits upon the throne will shelter them' (7.15). The earthly liturgies give way to the divine initiative, and from now on communion with God takes place without either mediation or ritual: God and the Lamb have taken charge of the festival on behalf of their people.

In thus referring to certain aspects of the Feast of Tabernacles, John adds a new colouring to the theme of the Exodus which runs through his book (paschal lamb, plagues of Egypt, song of Moses, etc.). In the light of the Exodus the resurrection of Christ is seen as the liberation and the salvation of a people. But the present situation of the churches addressed by John is also to be understood as the time of the stay in the wilderness: a period of testing and extreme vulnerability for the people, but also a period in which God multiplies signs of concern on tenderness towards them.

a multitude of brethren' and thus of the new people of God, has already been presented by John as being 'the lion of the tribe of Judah'. So we can understand why Judah is mentioned first among the sons of Jacob, even though it is not the oldest.

2. The omission of Dan is easily understood; it is because of the tribe's reputation for idolatry (see e.g. Judges 18 and above all the Jewish traditions about Dan). John excludes Dan from his list because of his very firm standpoint against any form of idolatry and in particular against emperor worship.

3. After Judah, Reuben regains to a degree its due place as the oldest, and is named before the other ten tribes.

4. However, the greatest novelty comes immediately after the mention of Reuben. We can see that John first refers to the sons of the servants of Jacob, and then gives the names of the sons borne by the legitimate wives of Jacob. This is incredible theological boldness, with which John reinterprets in a radically new way the origins of the people of God. What interests John is not Israel according to the flesh but a completely new Israel, in which the sons of the servants have as much dignity as the sons of the legitimate spouses.

So even in a list which seems so particularistic in its reference to the twelve tribes of Israel, John loudly affirms that the resurrection of Christ has done away with the differences and that the new people of God is founded, not on belonging according to the flesh, but on the infinite freedom of the God of Jesus Christ and the universal power of the resurrection of Christ.

nate; nant alumni petutate umcate, roffe de　　　cauit. lotus auit iste solitudinis est clauistre. de
bile siue imolat dño opus ño carreate mal　　　quo dict qui timent in tre siquid potct dñs
dñs auit iste regut gêteç i motus carnales inuic　　　pare silam i deserto. sic auit fatt dñs a deo

# 9

# The Battle of the Dragon with the Woman

## (Apocalypse 12)

Although this chapter fits easily into the extension of the heavenly signs mentioned in the last verses of Chapter 11, the appearance of a galaxy of new figures invites us to see it as a new section. These new figures are, in order of appearance: a woman clothed with the sun, the great red dragon, a male child, Michael and his angels, a great eagle, and other descendants of the woman. First of all let us see the identity of the main figures in this chapter. Then we will be in a better position to understand what is at stake in the battle in which they are engaged, and its outcome.

## The sign of the woman clothed with the sun

The liturgical use of Apocalypse 12 for the Feast of the Assumption of the Virgin Mary might suggest that a Mariological reading had priority. However, that is not the case. The earliest interpretations and those of present-day exegetes and in fact by far the majority of commentators down the centuries favour an ecclesiological interpretation.

There are many solid arguments for this:

1. The Old Testament often resorts to the figure of a woman to denote the whole people of God (Hosea 1–3; Isa. 26.17–28; 54; Micah 4.9–10; Ezek. 16 and 23; Song of Songs, etc.), and the New Testament does the same (Gal. 4; Eph. 5). John is taking up this two-fold tradition.

2. The 'twelve stars' which crown her head (12.1) again refer to the people of God, once founded on the twelve tribes of Israel and now on the twelve apostles.

3. Giving birth in anguish is associated in the Jewish tradition with Zion, which is also a symbol of the people of God.

4. The flight and the stay in the wilderness are difficult to apply to an episode from the life of Mary, whereas the duration of the stay clearly relates to the actual period of tribulation undergone by the church, either the 'one thousand two hundred and sixty days' (verse 6) or 'a time, times and half a time' (three and a half years forty-two months), which amounts to the same thing.

5. The divine protection in various forms (food and the help of the great eagle) evokes the protection which God had granted his people at the time of the Exodus and the stay in the desert. The mention of the archangel Michael is in the same vein, since in an apocalyptic tradition well known by John – the book of Daniel – he is presented as 'the great prince who has charge of your people', i.e. its protector (Dan. 12.1; cf. 10.13, 21). The figure of Michael also plays a dominant role in the unveiling and unfolding of the events of the end in non-canonical Jewish apocalypses.

6. John will take up the figure of the woman again indirectly in the features of the bride and

the wife (chapters 21–22) in relation to the new Jerusalem, which is itself presented in opposition to another woman, the harlot of chapter 17. Here we are always at the level of a community.

Does that mean that we must exclude all references to Mary? Not necessarily, but they must always be within an ecclesiological interpretation. Moreover that is a point which has always been important for those who hold to a Mariological exegesis of Apocalypse 12: they have never denied the primarily ecclesiological sense of the text. If they see a reference to Mary in it, it always remains secondary compared to the reference to the church.

In 12.5, for example, we have the birth of a male child who is the Messiah, and therefore Jesus the Christ. In this context it is probable, above all in a Johannine milieu, that the author would have thought of Mary the mother of Jesus. Furthermore we should remember that in the Gospel of John, the two times in which Jesus addresses his mother directly, he does so by using the mysterious and symbolic title 'woman' (John 2.4; 19.26). So it is not impossible that the author of the Apocalypse, who belonged to the Johannine circle, could have been alluding to Mary when he spoke of the woman clothed with the sun. We would then have Mary and the church superimposed on each other. Another argument invoked by those who adopt a Mariological interpretation is the certain reference in Apocalypse 12 to Genesis 3 – the mention of the old serpent. The reference is certain, but the question posed by modern exegesis in connection with Genesis 3.15 is whether we should see an individual or a communal figure here. The second interpretation tends to be uppermost. Be this as it may, in all the New Testament texts involving Mary, mother of Jesus, her place in the community of believers, and thus the mystery of the church, is always strongly emphasized, and here the features of the woman in Apocalypse 12 that one could apply to Mary are no exception.

## The dragon

Hardly has John introduced the figure of the woman than he presents us with a second sign, 'a great red dragon, with seven heads and ten horns, and seven diadems upon his heads' (12.3). He will be *the* antagonist; first he seeks to devour the male child born of the woman, and then the woman herself and her offspring. He himself is fought against, first by Michael and his angels (12.7ff.), and finally is mastered by 'an angel holding in his hand the key of the bottomless pit' (20.1) and is 'thrown (by God) into the lake of fire and brimstone . . . for ever and ever' (20.10).

But who is this dragon? First let's look at his attributes. The colour red indicates that he must be associated with the bloody forces already signalled with the second rider (6.4). Like the Beast who will soon appear (13.1), he is endowed with exceptional intelligence (seven heads – fullness of intelligence), and since each head has a diadem on it, he claims a certain royal power, while the 'ten horns' allude to the extent of his power. So he is a formidable adversary.

From a biblical perspective, the figure of the dragon, which has mythological connotations (see e.g. Isa. 27.1), has already been used in connection with legendary enemies of the people of God like the Pharaoh (Isa. 51.9; Ezek. 29.3; 32.2; Ps. 74.13–14) and Nebuchadnezzar (Jer. 51.34). Even if John goes still further in seeing the dragon as a representation of Satan, it is not impossible that he wanted to compare the present tribulation of the church with the two great tribulations attested in the Old Testament, the slavery in Egypt and the deportation to Babylon.

There is nothing surprising about such a transfer, since John himself resorts to many other images and titles to speak of the dragon: the old serpent (see Gen. 3), the devil or Satan, the deceiver of the whole world (12.9), and finally the accuser of our brethren (12.10). We are referred from the mythological domain to the historical domain, from the beginnings and the

# The Antichrist – an Apocalyptic Figure?

The Apocalypse is focussed on an imminent return of Christ. But to judge from Apocalypse 12–19 – and from the Synoptic apocalypse – such a return will not be unopposed. The forces of evil are at work in the world and present themselves in a very wide diversity of forms: dragon, beast, serpent, Satan, Babylon, etc.

Chapter 12 already gives us an impressive list of the titles given to Satan. But you will doubtless be surprised to learn that neither chapter 12 nor the following chapters use the word Antichrist. Contrary to widespread claims, some of them even put forward in dictionaries, the word Antichrist does not form any part of the vocabulary of the Apocalypse, nor is it part of the vocabulary of the Gospels.

In fact the term Antichrist is used by only one author in the New Testament: the author of the first two Letters of John (I John 21.18, 22; 4.3; II John 7 – there are five occurrences in all). Now the point of view of this author is extremely interesting:

1. He speaks of Antichrists in the plural. So there is no question of his wanting to reduce the Antichrist to a unique and singular being, or to make it a proper name.

2. Antichrist is more of a functional title, which John defines very clearly: 'Who is this liar but he who denies that Jesus is the Christ? This is the antichrist, he who denies the Father and the Son' (I John 2.22). In other words, in the end anyone can be Antichrist. Antichrist is anyone who rejects the Father and the Son. People would often like to identify a single Antichrist, as if he were responsible for all the evil in the world. But in defining the Antichrist so broadly, John invites each of us to examine our consciences seriously to see our connivance with evil and that in us which is opposed to Christ and his kingdom.

3. Is the Antichrist a figure related to the end of time? Everything depends on the sense one gives to the phrase 'the end of time'. The author of I John in fact speaks of the 'last hour', but we also have to see that for him this 'last hour' has already arrived. We are not necessarily referred to the end of time understood in the chronological sense, but to the days after the resurrection, when everyone has to declare for or against Christ: 'Children, it is the last hour; and as you have heard that antichrist is coming, so now many antichrists have come; therefore we know that it is the last hour' (I John 2.18).

So there can be no question of speculating on the existence of some monstrous and diabolical being who might be the Antichrist, and whose coming conditions that of Christ himself. The important thing is for our eyes to be fixed on the Christ who is coming. That is John's perspective in the Apocalypse; it has nothing to do with the figure of the Antichrist and again and always directs us towards the one Lord and Master of history: Christ, dead and risen.

heavenly world to the earthly world and the present situation of the world and of the church.

What more can be said in this connection? John presents him to us as a figure first belonging to the heavenly world (12.3) with other angels. But he and his angels are 'driven from heaven' (12.8) and 'thrown down to the earth' (12.9, 13). While his battle began in the heavenly world, it will end in the bottomless pit and the lake of fire (chapter 20); that will be his final defeat.

The dragon is not alone: in addition to his angels he also has in his service the Beast and the false prophet (the second Beast). However, while all are engaged in waging the same battle, they must not be confused. The Beast is not the dragon, and therefore is not Satan. The Beast belongs to the historical and human world. This distinction is very important, above all when we consider the efforts made in our day to bring the Apocalypse up to date and to find in contemporary history names which could be identified with the Beast. Extreme caution is needed in this kind of exercise, and it is certainly important to recall that the forces of evil at work in the world are not to be identified purely and simply with Satan (the dragon). Furthermore, it often happens that people talk of Antichrist in connection with chapters 12ff. of the Apocalypse; here again it is important to avoid over-hasty identifications, since the Apocalypse, like the Gospels, never uses the term Antichrist.

## The male child

Although it is only mentioned briefly, the figure of the male child appears as a great sign of hope and victory and gives us decisive orientation on the battle which the dragon is preparing to wage on the woman and her offspring: 'And the dragon stood before the woman who was about to bear a child, that he might devour her child when she brought it forth; she brought forth a male child, one who is to rule all the nations with a rod of iron, but her child was caught up to God and to his throne . . .' (12.4–6). The first object of the dragon's pursuit is the male child.

Who is this male child? The reference to Psalm 2.9 gives the passage a clearly messianic colouring. In John's perspective this is no unknown Messiah but Christ dead and risen, to whom he bears witness all through his book. Once more we must note how John has the gift of conveying the essentials to us. What he says about the male child refers to the two extreme poles of his existence: his birth and his raising up. There is not a single word about the public life and ministry of Christ. Furthermore, the allusion to the 'birth', the result of painful birthpangs, is to be understood in relation to the painful pangs of Calvary and thus to the death of Jesus rather than to his birth at Bethlehem. Did not Jesus himself present his death in terms of childbirth (John 16.19–22), and actually in the Apocalypse is he not designated the firstborn from the dead? So in a very condensed formula, John again presents to us the figure of Christ dead (his 'birth') and risen (he being 'caught up' to God and his throne).

## The battle with the dragon

War and battle come into the Apocalypse more than anywhere else in the New Testament (it has fifteen out of the twenty-five instances of 'war' and 'make war'). Chapter 12 gives us an earthly confrontation between Michael and his angels on the one side and the dragon and his angels on the other. This is a confrontation in which the Christians are involved. But it is simply the visible dimension of the battle which the Lamb has to wage against all the forces of evil (cf. 7.14; 19.19).

There is no doubt about the outcome of the battle. Even if we have to wait until chapter 20 to learn it, chapter 12 shows us that no matter how ferocious the attacks of the dragon may be, he is doomed to defeat. Thus in verse 8 we learn in connection with the dragon and his angels that 'they were defeated and there was no longer any place for them in heaven'. We can also see how the dragon is dominated, to the point of being 'thrown down' (the term is used four times) on earth. And finally, the canticle of verse 11 explicitly refers to the victory of Christians over the dragon.

Does that mean that everything is decided and that there is nothing more to fear? The last verse of the chapter reminds us that the war is not over and that the assaults of the dragon and his acolytes must still be resisted. However, the Christians who are now persecuted can take courage, since they know that the victory has been won by the Lamb and that they are preceded by a host of servants who have remained faithful to the Lamb and who with him have already gained the victory over the dragon.

## The 'beginning of the end' for the forces of evil

Whereas the section from chapter 12 to chapter 20 is recognized as the one in which the forces of evil appear to be most active, it is interesting to note how John introduces them one by one, and how he makes them disappear in turn, in total rout. The dragon himself and his associated forces disappear in reverse order to their appearance, as the following box indicates:

| Apocalypse 12–20 | | | | |
|---|---|---|---|---|
| A | B | C | B¹ | A¹ |
| Dragon (active) | Beasts (active) | Babylon (active and conquered) | Beasts (conquered) | Dragon (conquered) |
| ch. 12 | 13.1–14.5 | 14.5–19.10 | 19.11–21 | ch. 20 |

This is an ingenious procedure and is certainly deliberate. Thus the whole of the section is framed by the figure of the dragon (Satan). He is the one who has started the hostilities, and he is the most formidable opponent. He will also be the last to be conquered (ch. 20); only then can the victory of Christ be entire and definitive. In his service we shall see the successive appearance of the two beasts, who are historical figures, and who try to deceive the disciples of Christ and persecute them relentlessly (chs. 13–14). Just as their advent derives from the appearance of the dragon, so their rout immediately precedes and announces his imminent defeat (ch. 19). And finally, the third and last representation of evil, Babylon, whose fall is already announced in 14.8,

will be the first to experience the thunderbolts of judgment (chs. 17–18). By resorting to such a procedure, John creates a kind of dramatic tension: the assault of the forces of evil is presented, in descending order, in its most formidable forms (dragon – beasts – Babylon), while judgment is passed in ascending order, finally reaching the most formidable adversary (Babylon – beasts – dragon).

## A song of victory (vv. 10–12)

There is nothing reassuring about the vision of the dragon and its attacks, and the chapters which follow will show the extent to which he and his allies can ravage the earth, at least for a time. However, as he does so often elsewhere, John introduces a very strong christological note in the hymn contained in vv. 10–12, the function of which is to interpret the vision. Now the interpretation which he gives us is once more centred on the victory of the risen Christ: 'Now the salvation and the power and the kingdom of our God and the authority of his Christ have come . . .' (12.10). John applies to the Christ an attribute which the Beast will claim several times (seven times in chapters 13–17): authority (Greek *exousia*), i.e. Lordship. This is an attribute which the rest of the New Testament associates with the resurrection (Matt. 28; Acts 2.36; Phil. 2.9–10).

The hymn also celebrates the victory of the Christians: 'And they have conquered him by the blood of the Lamb and by the word of their testimony, for they loved not their lives even unto death' (12.11). Though some of them did not succeed in resisting to the end (cf.13.7–8), John can already bear witness to the fact that a large number of them had the courage to follow their master to the end, and chose to pass through death to achieve life.

Finally, the hymn ends with a call to rejoice which echoes the psalms of the 'Kingdom of Yahweh' (93–96; 98), where the creative act of God is seen as a victory over the primordial forces of chaos. We can already see a profile of the new creation, the fruit of the victory of the Risen Christ over the dragon and the forces of evil and death.

# 10

# From the 'End of the World' to a New Creation

### (Apocalypse 21–22)

### Like a stained-glass window

Apocalypse 21–22 are among the finest pages of the whole Bible. Apart from a few verses (five in all) which utter the severest prophetic warnings, these two chapters are like an immense stained-glass window, with themes and colours opening on the infinite, and constantly lit by a blazing sun. John has already accustomed us to highly-coloured frescoes inspired by an unfailing hope. But this time he attains unprecedented heights, and gives us an extremely powerful and rich vision of the advent of a new world.

### The 'end' has already come!

It is certainly logical to expect the last chapters of John's work to speak to us of events of the 'end'. But is that the case? And do we really have to wait for the 'end' of John's book to hear of them?

In fact John has taken care to put all the elements in place so that in these last two chapters he can speak not so much of 'the end' itself but of what lies beyond 'the end'. While chapters 21–22 conclude his book as a whole, they also present us, in the clearest possible terms, with the outcome of the battle which has been described since chapter 12. And although this battle has been one of the most relentless, and accompanied with formidable scourges, it has to be said that the domination of the Beast

has been quite ephemeral: only chapter 13 concedes him some victories. All the other intermediary chapters (14–20) speak in one way or another of judgment, or the ruin and defeat of the dragon, his associates and his partisans. They also mark, each in its own way, the 'end of a world'. Before presenting us with his vision of the new and definitive world which will emerge from the hands of the God who has created the universe and raised Jesus from the dead, John assures us that the world of the Bible is doomed to failure and ruin.

### Beyond the 'end', a new world

The interpretation of the first twenty chapters of the Apocalypse which has already been given has kept us essentially at the level of history contemporaneous with John. The presentation of the five interpretative keys and the study of the texts has constantly led us to distinguish between apocalypse and the end of the world, and above all to understand that the main subject of John's Apocalypse is not the end of the world pure and simple. On the contrary, as we have seen, John's great preoccupation is to interpret present history in the light of a single event which has already taken place and which from now on gives meaning to the whole of human history: the resurrection of Christ.

But what about chapters 21–22? Must we not

say that their central aim is to describe what we are accustomed to call the end of the world? Our answer to this question must be qualified. John works with images and at no point gives an objective and realistic description of an event which might be called 'the end of the world'. Even in chapters 21–22 we look in vain for a concrete scenario and a chronological description of the events of the end. It would be more precise to say that John assumes the end as already having come, rather than describing it. His attention is directed elsewhere, beyond the end, to the radically new world that God is shaping for humankind.

On the other hand, one can never emphasize enough how this world is new: new heaven, new earth, new Jerusalem, new universe. This is no superficial rearrangement, nor a cyclical return of things, but profound, radical newness. John's vocabulary is very significant in this respect. Writing in Greek, he can use two adjectives to speak of what is new, *neos* (as in neologism) and *kainos* (for which there is no English equivalent). The former refers to chronological newness: what is more recent, what has just appeared in time. But this is not the term that John has kept. He exclusively uses the second adjective to bring out the qualitative dimension of the newness: it is of a different order, radically new.

There are scholars who would argue that John is interested only in the first coming of Christ and nowhere speaks of the end of the world, and put forward this view passionately. And of course we have to define what is meant by the 'first heaven' and 'first earth' and the 'old world'. But there can surely be no doubt that the visions of John point us beyond present history to a radically different world from the one we know, since it will be freed from all forms of suffering, death and curse.

## The model of a stained-glass window

The beautiful window of the New Jerusalem has been skilfully conceived and assembled by John.

Before we admire its details, let's consider the model of chapters 21–22.

John first gives us three parallel sections (21.1–8; 21.9–27; 22.1–5) which describe with different images the same reality: the new Jerusalem, the holy city. This first block is followed by a vision (22.6–15) which echoes the inaugural vision in 1.9–20 and is centred on the imminent return of Christ, while the epilogue (22.16–21) is constructed on the form of a dialogue between Christ and his church.

The parallelism of the first three sections is marked by the return of three elements:

1. John is given *a vision* through a heavenly being and can hear a voice which already gives him an interpretation of the vision:

'Then I saw a new heaven and a new earth; for the first heaven and the first earth had passed away, and the sea was no more. And I saw the holy city, new Jerusalem, coming down out of heaven from God, prepared as a bride adorned for her husband; and I heard a great voice from the throne saying, "Behold, the dwelling of God is with men. He will dwell with them, and they shall be his people, and God himself will be with them"' (21.1–3).

'Then came one of the seven angels who had the seven bowls full of the seven last plagues, and spoke to me, saying, "Come, I will show you the Bride, the wife of the Lamb." And in the Spirit he carried me away to a great, high mountain, and showed me the holy city Jerusalem coming down out of heaven from God' (21.9–10).

'Then the angel showed me the river of life, bright as crystal, flowing from the throne of God and of the Lamb' (22.1).

2. Then comes *the description of the holy city*, 'the dwelling of God with men . . .' (21.3), resplendent and superbly constructed with 'twelve gates, and at the gates twelve angels, and on the gates the names of the twelve tribes of the sons of Israel were inscribed' (21.12), and a wall which had 'twelve foundations, and on them the twelve names of the twelve apostles of the

Lamb' (21.14). In the centre is the 'throne of God and of the Lamb', from which flows 'the river of Life' (22.1), which transforms the city and the garden, whose fruits are renewed eternally: 'Through the middle of the street of the city, on either side of the river, the tree of life with its twelve kinds of fruit, yielding its fruit each month; and the leaves of the tree were for the healing of the nations' (22.2).

3. At the end of each of these visions *a severe warning* rings out, which sometimes borders on an excommunication (21.8; 21.27; 22.15). While these warnings do not in any way detract from the beauty of the visions reported by John, they do put the readers in a position of freedom and responsibility. The new Jerusalem remains the object of a free choice, and the salvation freely offered carries with it very high demands for conversion.

## From Babylon to Jerusalem . . . or from lamentations to glorification

The great vision of chapters 21–22 has been skilfully prepared for by John. So far he has been more than discreet about Jerusalem. It is envisaged in 11.8, while the holy city which can also claim the title of great city is 'symbolically' called Sodom or Egypt. This is the only historical reminiscence which John gives us of the city of Jerusalem. Here as in 2.12 he is interested in the *new* Jerusalem. By contrast, he has paid much more attention to Babylon (= Rome), the arrogant and oppressive city whose activities have already been described in chapter 13, and then spelt out in more detail in chapters 17–18.

However, whereas chapters 17–18 announce the decline and punishment of Babylon, John takes up the same words or their opposite this time to spell out the exaltation of Jerusalem. The hour is no longer one of mourning but of rejoicing and of wedding festivities. So two great cities come face to face in the Apocalypse and are as it were diametrically opposed.

The table on the next page allows us to see the many parallels and contrasts established by the author between Babylon and Jerusalem.

Several times in the course of the present study I have emphasized how John loved to work with two strokes in succession, and how his procedure is often to speak twice of the same reality (for example the two parts of chapter 7, or the 144,000 in chapters 7 and 14). This time, as I indicated earlier, John's procedure is three-fold (21.1–8; 21.9–27; 22.1–5). Again drawing on a wide variety of images and motifs, he develops the same fundamental theme, that of the holy city (2.2, 10), this city in which 'the throne of God and of the Lamb' will stand (22.3) and which he identifies as the new Jerusalem (21.2, 10). This is not a simple repetition. On the contrary, each time John explores more deeply a facet of what will be the holy city.

### Jerusalem, new humanity (21.1–8)

First, one could say that John is interested in the human and relational dimension of the new Jerusalem. Whether one speaks of eternal life or the kingdom of heaven or of paradise or of the holy city, or imagines quite a different way of talking of the other world, the essential thing will always be the advent of this new humanity, freed from all hindrances to happiness, and engaged in full and living communion with God.

While John is speaking of a city, he immediately compares it with 'a bride adorned for her husband' (21.2). This nuptial image is reinforced and developed by verses 2 and 3, which describe in exceptional terms the presence of God with all humanity and the reciprocal relationship which will henceforth exist between them: 'Behold, the dwelling of God is with men. He will dwell with them, and they shall be his people, and God himself will be with them.' Better still, God will eliminate for good what makes humanity so vulnerable and causes it such suffering: 'He will wipe away every tear from their eyes, and death shall be no more, neither shall there be mourning nor crying nor pain any more . . .' (21.4). In other words, for John, the new world that God is

# From Lamentations to Glorification
## Apocalypse 17 and 21–22

| Babylon | New Jerusalem |
|---|---|
| Seventh bowl: destruction of Babylon (16.17–21) | [seventh vision]: descent of Jerusalem (21.1–18) |
| One of the seven angels approaches (17.1) | One of the seven angels approaches (21.9) |
| Invitation, 'Come, I will show you . . .' (17.1) | Invitation, 'Come, I will show you . . .' (21.9) |
| The great harlot (17.1) | The bride, the wife of the Lamb (21.9) |
| 'And he carried me away in the Spirit into a wilderness' (17.3) | 'And in the Spirit he carried me away to a great, high mountain' (21.10) |
| Beginning of the vision (17.3b) | Beginning of the vision (21.10b) |
| 'The woman was arrayed in purple and scarlet, and bedecked with gold and jewels and pearls, holding in her hand a golden cup full of abominations and the impurities of her fornication' (17.4) | 'As a bride adorned for her husband . . .' (21.2)<br><br>'Having the glory of God, its radiance like a most rare jewel, like a jasper, clear as crystal' (21.11) |
| 'It has become a dwelling place of demons, a haunt of every foul spirit, a haunt of every foul and hateful bird' (18.2) | 'Behold, the dwelling of God is with men. He will dwell with them . . .' (21.3) |
| 'The waters that you saw, where the harlot is seated, are peoples and multitudes and nations and tongues. And the ten horns that you saw, they and the beast will hate the harlot; they will make her desolate and naked, and devour her flesh and burn her up with fire' (17.15–16) | 'By its light shall the nations walk; and the kings of the earth shall bring their glory into it. . . . they shall bring into it the glory and the honour of the nations' (21.24, 26) |
| 'It has become a dwelling place of demons, a haunt of every foul spirit, a haunt of every foul and hateful bird' (18.2) | 'But nothing unclean shall enter it, nor any one who practises abomination or falsehood . . .' (21.27) |
| 'And the dwellers on earth whose names have not been written in the book of life from the foundation of the world, will marvel to behold the beast' (17.8) | 'Only those who are written in the Lamb's book of life shall enter it' (21.27) |
| Babylon is doomed to destruction (18.8) | In the city, the servants of God 'shall reign for ever and ever' (22.5) |
| Babylon, 'bedecked with gold, with jewels, and with pearls', is devastated (18.16–17) | 'She (Bride = Jerusalem) has the glory of God, its radiance like a most rare jewel, like a jasper, clear as crystal' (21.11) |

preparing is not something 'in itself' but a world of communion and infinite happiness for humankind. In speaking of what will take place 'beyond the end', John is not speaking of a place or of inanimate objects, but of persons and relationships: 'I will be his God and he shall be my son' (21.7).

The whole of this first series of affirmations goes beyond a purely metaphorical level. There is nothing approximate about them, nor do they require to be decoded, since they speak to us directly of the essential mystery of the beyond, regardless of whatever name we give it – heaven, paradise or kingdom: a harmonious relationship and a profound communion between God and humankind.

## Jerusalem, a city resplendent with the glory of God

Pursuing his contemplation of the holy city, John now draws on a new kind of language, which is more metaphorical. This time he speaks of precious stones, gates and walls, and measures. All these are images which bear witness to the splendour and perfection of the city. But what makes the splendour and radiance of the city if not the fact that it has 'the glory of God' (21.11)?

Verses 15–17 recall the actions which Ezekiel was once ordered to perform (Ezek.40–48), namely to measure the temple and the city in which the glory of God dwells. The measures provided by John are ideal: the holy city is perfect at every point. But the most amazing thing is that the same action can no longer be applied to the temple, since mediation is rendered obsolete by the direct and immediate presence of God and the Lamb: 'And I saw no temple in the city, for its temple is the Lord God the Almighty and the Lamb' (21.22).

There is no temple, but there is worship and pilgrimage. Jerusalem is an ever-open city, open to the 'nations' and to the 'kings of the earth'. So in the second stage of his reflections, John has been able to be precise about the notion of worship, which will no longer relate to particular places and times but will be in the joy and splendour of a light which shines endlessly in the eyes of all humankind.

## Jerusalem, garden of life

Finally, John has yet more surprises for us. The second section of his stained-glass window offered us schematic and largely rigid features; the city had walls and solid – and to a degree static – foundations. But now, suddenly, John begins to talk of a 'river of life' and of 'trees of life' (22.1–2) and of leaves and fruits. So we are back in the original garden (Genesis 2–3) without the prohibitions and the curse. On the contrary, there is no darkness and a superabundance of life. Humanity does not in any way compete with the world of God. God is recognized as God, and humanity can now enter fully into the world of God and reign with God: 'They need no light of lamp or sun, for the Lord God will be their light, and they shall reign for ever and ever' (22.5).

## An admirable biblical synthesis

No doubt John was unaware that he was writing the last pages of the New Testament and indeed of the whole Bible. It was the Christian communities which, while fixing the canon and the order of the biblical books, put his book right at the end of the Bible. We can only congratulate ourselves today and recognize that they were certainly inspired to do this. As a result, Apocalypse 21–22 appears as the culminating point, the keystone, of the great millenary work that we call the Bible. A large number of major themes are crowned and consecrated in it: *new creation, new Israel, new covenant, new temple, eternal nuptials between God and his people*, and so on.

*New creation, new genesis.* In fact the word of God, sovereign and creative, resounds with the same solemnity and power as in the first chapters of Genesis: 'And he who sat upon the throne said, "Behold, I make all things new"' (21.5). Not only do we once again find the garden and tree of life, this time with neither serpent nor

snare, but water flows in abundance and the trees do not cease to produce fruit for the utmost wellbeing of humankind.

*New Israel, new Jerusalem.* Psalm 122, like the other Psalms of Ascent (120–134), well expresses the place occupied by Jerusalem in the hearts of Jewish believers. It was around Jerusalem that the believers of the Old Testament built their most foolish hopes of peace and happiness. But we also know how Jerusalem multiplied its infidelities (to the point of being called Sodom and Egypt in the Apocalypse), and how it often experienced the tragedy of wars and invasions, particularly in the decade or decades preceding the composition of the Apocalypse. Now John shows it to us resplendent and open for the nations to stream into. Faithful to his promise, God makes it the place for the gathering of the tribes of Israel, but from now on Israel no longer knows any frontiers. The people of God finally appears in its definitive form, since God gathers together his peoples.

*New covenant.* 'I will be your God and you shall be my people' is one of the most characteristic formulations of the covenant. It is taken up again here in new terms: 'They shall be his people, and God himself will be with them and be their God' (21.3). As in the days of the Burning Bush and Sinai, God reveals himself as Emmanuel, that is to say as the God who goes with his people and unveils himself progressively by intervening on their behalf.

*New temple.* John shows remarkable boldness in his description of the holy city. Whereas Jewish hope attached so much importance to the rebuilding of the temple, John announces that there will no longer be any occasion for human and ritual mediation: 'And I saw no temple in the city, for its temple is the Lord God the Almighty and the Lamb. And the city has no need of sun or moon to shine upon it, for the glory of God is its light, and its lamp is the Lamb' (21.22–23).

*Eternal nuptials between God and his people.* This is the finest image we are given anywhere in the Bible to express the relations between God and his people. It comes from the prophet Hosea (1–3): God is the husband who loves passionately, madly and unconditionally but whose love is constantly reborn by the offering of tenderness and mercy. This refrain of the marriage between God and his people is taken up often in the prophetic tradition and in the teaching of Jesus, and here finds its consecration: the 'bride' is 'adorned for her husband' (2.34). It is the 'Bride, the wife of the Lamb' (21.9) who henceforward expects the return of the Lamb, which she calls for with all her might in communion with the Spirit: 'The Spirit and the Bride say, "Come!"' (22.17).

# THE LAST WORD

At the beginning of our reading of the Apocalypse I noted the 'apocalyptic' disquiet which has marked the last two decades. Now that we are in the decade which will end in the year 2000, the tension is even greater. For many people, there is something fateful about this date. Very recently the Gulf War revived such disquiet, and we could hear both sides conjuring up an 'apocalyptic' scenario, each one regarding the other as Satan or accusing it of diabolical manoeuvres.

At the height of the crisis, when it was still uncertain what turn the conflict would take, I was asked to take part in a phone-in programme in which people were asked to comment on the possibility of an imminent end to the world. For the event, the producers had prepared a brief documentary surveying the biblical 'prophecies' (Ezekiel, Daniel and the Apocalypse of John), read in the fundamentalist manner of Hal Lindsey, and the 'prophecies' of Nostradamus. The main question raised by the audience was whether or not Armageddon would soon be upon us.

This broadcast made me aware how far fundamentalist readings are still widespread among the general public. A large number of hearers, claiming the support of the Bible, said that they were convinced of the imminence of Christ's return. To desire Christ's return is one thing, but to say with certainty that it is imminent is another!

The fundamentalist readings which interpret the current international political situation in the light of the Bible use two major arguments, taken more or less directly from authors like Hal Lindsey. The first of them is that all the prophecies of the Old Testament relating to the first coming of the Messiah were fulfilled precisely. So those relating to his second coming will be fulfilled with the same precision. Now a careful reading of the New Testament would lead us to quite a different interpretation of the fulfilment of prophecies. Far from claiming that these prophecies were fulfilled literally and in detail, the New Testament authors do not hesitate to introduce changes into the text or the interpretation of the ancient prophecies by reason of the new things which have come to pass in Jesus. Jesus fulfils the scriptures, but often in an unexpected way, and always with added meaning. So we must not try to establish equivalences of a mathematical kind. What is important is the meaning of the events which people attempt to shed light on by bringing up to date the ancient words of the prophets.

A second argument relates to the meaning one gives to the word Israel. In the wake of Hal Lindsey and others like him, a large number of those involved in this radio programme were absolutely convinced that the conditions for an imminent return of Christ are already in place. For them, one of these fundamental conditions is the relatively recent fact of the creation of the state of Israel. Since the majority of the biblical apocalyptic texts speak of a final assault on Israel, there is a risk that possible dates of the end of the world will be given on the basis of any conflict in which Israel is implicated. However, for both the Apocalypse and the whole of the New Testament, it is clear that the word Israel has primarily a theological value: it is a way of denoting the people of God, and not a clearly-defined political territory. There was no state of Israel in the time of Ezekiel, Daniel or John! So it is wrong to make extrapolations from what has become the modern state of Israel to determine the time and manner of the end.

It is impossible to emphasize too strongly the importance, not to say the urgency, of reading the Apocalypse of John and putting it in perspective. We recognized at the start the difficulties and risks of such an enterprise. The Apocalypse of John is not one of those books which one can boast of having mastered. On the contrary, it is a book that one can never shut, any more than one can claim to have heard the last word of revelation. The 'last word' in the Apocalypse is, in fact, about beginning and beginning again: 'Amen. Come, Lord Jesus! The grace of the Lord Jesus be with all the saints. Amen' (22.21).

This two-fold 'Amen' defines in a remarkable way the two poles of Christian existence. Since the Risen Christ is the Alpha and Omega, the principle of a new world, we say 'Amen' to the future: 'Come, Lord Jesus.' But to say 'Amen' to the future is not to switch off or resign from the present. We also say 'Amen' to the present, welcoming it as an event of grace: 'The grace of the Lord Jesus be with all the saints.' It is here and now that we must bear witness to the hope that inspires us.

# How to Study the Rest of the Apocalypse

- **Apocalypse 1**: This chapter is dominated by the figure of a son of man whose titles coincide with those of Christ. To appreciate this chapter better you might therefore refer to the first key for reading, presented under the title 'Discovering the Christ of the Apocalypse'.

- **Apocalypse 8–9 and Apocalypse 16** have the same structure and theological orientation as Apocalypse 6–7. So consult the chapter 'From Judgment to Salvation'.

- **Apocalypse 10–11** serve as an interlude (a vision of hope) before the seventh trumpet sounds. Whereas the symbolism of the book up to chapter 10 does not pose any major problems, chapter 11 is worth deep study: the role of the two witnesses is particularly significant for the mission of Christian communities in the world.

- **Apocalypse 13**: You will in fact find all the elements needed to interpret this famous passage in the two chapters of the first part which discuss the historical context ('Reading Prophecy for the Present') and the symbolic dimension ('The Apocalypse in Figures and Colours').

- **Apocalypse 14**: With its two-fold image of harvest and wine harvest, this chapter would have much to offer towards understanding the theme of judgment. I would stress that judgment is first announced as 'an eternal gospel to proclaim to those that dwell on earth' (v. 6), the ultimate object of which is to bring about the glorification and adoration of the faithful.

- **Apocalypse 15**: With only eight verses, this chapter poses no problems. The song of the Lamb leads us to celebrate the mighty acts of a God of deliverance, as Moses did after the crossing of the Red Sea. This chapter, too, is an interlude, and offers a glimpse of the final victory before the seven bowls of the wrath of God are poured out.

- **Apocalypse 17–18**: chapter 17 is clearly parallel to chapter 13, and explains its main symbols; chapter 18 is a funeral lament over Babylon (Rome), a lament many features of which will be taken up, in an opposite or changed form, in the hymn of joy over the new Jerusalem (see the chapter 'From the "End of the World" to a New Creation').

- **Apocalypse 19–20**: These two chapters of battle are dominated by the figure of Christ and devoted to the celebration of his final victory over the dragon and the Beast. For the thousand years of chapter 20 see pages 33ff. above.

# FOR FURTHER READING

*Introduction*

A. Yarbro Collins, 'Reading the Book of Revelation in the Twentieth Century', *Interpretation. A Journal of Bible and Theology* 40, 1986, 229–42.

*Chapter 2*

A. Yarbro Collins, 'The Political Perspective of the Revelation to John', *Journal of Biblical Literature* 96, 241–56

A. Yarbro Collins, 'The Revelation of John: An Apocalyptic Response to a Social Crisis', *Currents in Theology and Mission* 8, 1981, 4–12

A. Yarbro Collins, *Christ and Catharsis: The Power of the Apocalypse*, Westminster Press 1984

*Chapter 3*

There is no recent work for the systematic study of the symbols of the Apocalypse and the biblical symbols generally. Refer to the detailed exegesis of a particular passage in the major commentaries. Recent monographs on the symbolism of numbers present developments in kabbalistic interpretation.

I. Abrahams, 'Numbers, Typical and Important', *Encyclopaedia Judaica* 12, Jerusalem 1972, 1254–61

*Chapter 4*

*Texts of other apocalypses*

*The Old Testament Pseudepigrapha*, ed. James H. Charlesworth, Doubleday and Darton, Longman and Todd 1983, 1985 (two volumes): Vol. 1 contains the Apocalyptic Literature and Testaments, Vol. 2 contains expansions of Old Testament books, Legends, Wisdom, etc. (and includes the Book of Jubilees)

*The Apocryphal Old Testament*, ed. H. F. D. Sparks, Clarendon Press 1984

Geza Vermes, *The Dead Sea Scrolls in English*, Penguin Books ³1987

*Books on apocalyptic*

P. D. Hanson, *The Dawn of Apocalyptic*, Fortress Press 1975

—— , *Old Testament Apocalyptic*, Abingdon Press 1987

Christopher Rowland, *The Open Heaven*, SPCK and Crossroad Publishing Company 1982

H. H. Rowley, *The Relevance of Apocalyptic*, Lutterworth Press ³1963

D. S. Russell, *Apocalyptic Ancient and Modern*, SCM Press 1978

—— , *Divine Disclosure*, SCM Press and Fortress Press 1992

*Chapter 6*

D. E. Aune, 'The Form and Function of the Proclamations to the Seven Churches (Revelation 2–3)', *New Testament Studies* 26, 1990, 182–204

C. J. Hemer, *The Letters to the Seven Churches of Asia in their Local Setting*, JSOT Press 1986

W. H. Shea, 'The Covenantal Form of the Letters to the Seven Churches', *Andrews University Seminary Studies* 21, 1983, 71–84

*Chapter 7*

R. Bauckham, 'The Eschatological Earthquake in the Apocalypse of John', *Novum Testamentum* 19, 1977, 224–33

L. W. Hurtado, 'Revelation 4–5 in the Light of Jewish Apocalyptic Analogies', *Journal for the Study of the New Testament* 25, 1985, 105–24

C. Rowland, 'The Visions of God in Apocalyptic Literature', *Journal for the Study of Judaism* 10, 1979, 137–54

W. C. Van Unnik, '"Worthy is the Lamb". The Background of Apocalypse 5', in *Mélanges bibliques en hommage au R. P. Béda Rigaux*, Duculot, Gembloux 1970, 445–61

*Chapter 8*

J. A. Draper, 'The Feast of Tabernacles: Revelation 7.1–17', *Journal for the Study of the New Testament* 19, 1983, 133–47

H. Ulpgard, *Feast and Future. Revelation 7.9–17 and the Feast of Tabernacles*, Coniectanea Biblica, New Testament Series 22, Almquist and Wiksell, Lund 1989

C. R. Smith, 'The Portrayal of the Church as the New Israel in the Names and Order of the Tribes in Revelation 7.5–8', *Journal for the Study of the New Testament* 39, 1990, 111–18

*On the structure of Apocalypse 4.1–22.5*

E. Schüssler Fiorenza, 'Composition and Structure of the Book of Revelation', *Catholic Biblical Quarterly* 39, 1977, 344–66

*Chapter 9*

R. D. Aus, 'The Relevance of Isaiah 66.7 to Revelation 12 and II Thessalonians 1', *Zeitschrift für die Neutestamentliche Wissenschaft und die Kunde der Alteren Kirche* 67, 1976, 252–68

E. Testa, 'The Woman in Revelation 12', in *Mary in the New Testament*, Fortress Press 1978, 219–39

A. Yarbro Collins, *The Combat Myth in the Book of Revelation*, Harvard Dissertations in Religion 9, Scholars Press, Missoula, Montana 1976

*Chapter 10*

D. E. Aune, 'The Prophetic Circle of John of Patmos and the Exegesis of Revelation 22.16', *Journal for the Study of the New Testament* 37, 1989, 103–16

T. Collins, *Apocalypse 22.6–21 as the Focal Point of Moral Teaching and Exhortation in the Apocalypse*, Pontifical Gregorian University, Rome 1986

C. Deutsch, 'Transformation of Symbols: The New Jerusalem in Revelation 21, 1–22, 5', *Zeitschrift für die Neutestamentliche Wissenschaft und die Kunde der Alteren Kirche* 78, 1987, 106–26

W. J. Dumbrell, *The End of the Beginning: Revelation 21–22 and the Old Testament*, Lancer Books, Homebush West 1985

R. H. Gundry, 'The New Jerusalem: People as Place, not Place for People', *Novum Testamentum* 29, 1987, 254–64

U. Jart, 'The Precious Stones in the Revelation of St John xxi, 18–21', *Studia Theologica* 24, 1970, 150–81

*A Selective General Bibliography*

1. Commentaries

J. M. Ford, *Revelation*, The Anchor Bible, Doubleday 1981

L. Morris, *The Revelation of St John*, Tyndale New Testament Commentaries, Inter-Varsity Press and Eerdmans 1983

R. H. Mounce, *The Book of Revelation*, New International Commentary on the New Testament, Eerdmans 1977

E. Schüssler Fiorenza, *The Book of Revelation: Justice and Judgment*, Fortress Press 1985

J. P. M. Sweet, *Revelation*, SCM Press 1979

A. Yarbro Collins, 'The Apocalypse', in *The New Jerome Biblical Commentary*, ed. R. E. Brown, J. A. Fitzmyer and R. E. Murphy, Prentice-Hall and Geoffrey Chapman 1990, 996–1116

——, *Crisis and Catharsis: The Power of the Apocalypse*, Westminster Press 1984

2. Introductions and Other Accounts of General Interest

R. Bauckham, 'The Worship of Jesus in Apocalyptic Christianity', *New Testament Studies* 27, 1981, 322–41

M. D. Goulder, 'The Apocalypse as an Annual Cycle of Prophecies', *New Testament Studies* 27, 1981, 342–67

D. Guthrie, *The Relevance of John's Apocalypse*, Paternoster Press and Eerdmans 1987

R. L. Jeske, 'Spirit and Community in the Johannine Apocalypse', *New Testament Studies* 31, 1985, 452–66

A. Yarbro Collins, 'Oppression from Without: The Symbolization of Rome as Evil in Early Christianity', in *Truth and Its Victims*, Concilium 200, 1988, 79–88